Educational Thinkers

V.R. Taneja
S. Taneja

ATLANTIC
PUBLISHERS & DISTRIBUTORS (P) LTD

Published by

ATLANTIC

PUBLISHERS & DISTRIBUTORS (P) LTD

7/22, Ansari Road, Darya Ganj, New Delhi-110002
Phones : +91-11-40775252, 40775214, 23273880, 23275880
Fax: +91-11-23285873
Web: www.atlanticbooks.com
E-mail: orders@atlanticbooks.com

Reprint 2006, 2011, 2021, 2022, 2023

Printed & bound in India by Atlantic Print Services

Preface

A textbook continues to be one of the major variables that vitally conditions the teaching-learning process. It generates educative interactions between the learner and the learner, as also between the learner and the teacher. It may be used for learning in advance of the classroom instructions, for enriching the learning, for revision and reinforcement of the previous learning. The merit and utility of understanding the educational thoughts and practices of the masterminds (both Western and Indian) cannot be overemphasised. This is the *raison d'etre* of this book, which is written with experience-centred approach.

V.R. TANEJA
S. TANEJA

Contents

1

Plato

(427 B.C. TO 347 B.C.)

Born in Greece in May 427 B.C. Plato, at the age of 20 years became the disciple of Socrates, who was at that time over 60 years. Plato remained a bachelor all through his life and remained dedicated in preaching the ideas of Socrates. It is said that "if Socrates created the song of philosophy, it was Plato, who sang the tune". To the world, Plato has bequeathed three things: (1) Theory of a new form of Government, called Republic; (2) A new Social Order; and (3) A well-articulated system of Education. He considered all these three as "the grandest and most beautiful subjects". Of these three he deemed education "as the first and fairest thing that the best of men can ever have". He has expanded his thoughts and practice of education in his two books, entitled the *Republic* and the *Laws*. Though the title — Republic — gives the idea of being a treatise on politics, it abounds Plato's thoughts on education, which were slightly modified in the Laws, which book he wrote in old age. His book Republic is highly appreciated by Rousseau in the words, "if you wish to know what is meant by public education, read Plato's *Republic.*"

His Philosophy

Plato was humanistically idealist. In his *Republic* he has visualised an ideal State, where Justice should reign supreme. He viewed the world with an open mind and propounded the philosophy of Idealism, which has influenced political science, religion and education since his times to the present day. Although he has given many lofty ideas and ideals but does not impose them and wants that every individual should know them and accept them only if he is convinced about the merit and virtue of those ideas and ideals.

In his books — the *Republic* and the *Laws*, he has given first place to the State and second place to the individual. Since the individual has many wants, which he may not be able to get through his own efforts, State is in a position to provide these wants to the individual. If the State, he averred, functioned in a perfect manner, the individuals would lead good life because the "State is a divine agency with a divine function, which realises the Good upon the earth after the model of absolute justice. The State has ethical aims". Even family was denigrated by Plato in comparison to the State, which was considered paramount and he "recommended State control of the breeding, nursing and training of children". He permitted "family life only to the slaves". The state, he said, is absolutely supreme.

In the context of education, a philosopher's thinking is understood in terms of five parameters, *viz.* his concept of Reality, Man, Mind, Knowledge and Values.

In the domain of Reality, Plato said that man lives in two worlds — the world of senses and the world of ideas. He called the world of senses as the material world, which has nothing perfect, nothing permanent, In this world everything is in space and time. Everything is subject to change Every material thing is a copy or the shadow of the real and is the source of all evil, the cause of all imperfections.

On the other hand the ideal Reality is the world of ideas, which is the mind of God. Things of the earth are modelled on these ideas, This world is eternal, spaceless and not subject to change. It is the world of mind, a world of abstract thought. The ideas are interrelated in a divine order or perfect mind. According to Plato the *true reality* is thought or an idea, the realisation of winch leads to spiritual bliss, Since he exalts the world of ideas, he is called an Idealist and his philosophy is called idealism. He urged the human-beings to convert the life of senses to the love of ideal reality. This was possible through the rational faculty of man. The soul should be turned from low" interests to high interests. He commended the turning of soul passing from a day (which is better than night) to the true day of being", that is one should go on ascending from below upward. This, he said, can be done by studying arithmetic, which "has a very great elevating effect, compelling the soul to reason about abstract numbers, and rebelling against the introduction of visible objects into the argument."

Plato believed that "Good" was the highest reality and in order to be a moral man, one must possess certain virtues or "Goods of the Soul" like justice, self-control, magnanimity or temperance.

Regarding his concept of MAN, he was humanist to the core and regards man as the epitome of the universe having two elements — the soul and the body, the two distinct and separate entities. According to him Soul has three parts: (1) instincts, drives, appetites, desires etc. and (2) Courage or spirit, which inspires endurance, hardihood and perseverance. These two belong to the body and are subject to decay and destruction. The appetites, therefore, should be curbed. The third is the *reason*, which is divine, and is not related to body but is the function of the head. Body, he said, deprives the reason and is the source of all evil. Reason should decide things all the time. This is what Plato expected from man.

To him the "children are the riches and upon their turning out well or ill depends the whole order of their father's house". He affirms, "No one should bring children into the world who is unwilling to preserve to end their nurture and education". Since at birth the child is a creature of low appetites, he must be taught to rise above these and love the ideal rather than the actual.

He was an ardent lover of young men and wanted to gauge their mind. To him the secret of virtue lay in the desire for right things. Our true nature is fully operative in loving the good and aspiring for that. Efforts should be made to lead a good life. 'The function of education is to prepare for and accelerate these efforts, It will be of no avail if there is no exacting love for the goal. This is Platonic love, which is based on positive rationalism and passionate empiricism.

Plato recognised two kinds of MIND, the empirical and the rational The empirical mind begins from the parts and proceeds to the whole, while the rational mind begins from the whole and moves towards the parts. Being an idealist he placed 'the whole' above the 'parts' and considered "ends" more important than the "means".

His theory that ideas are innate and already exist in the mind led him to assert that all knowledge is anamensis (reminiscence), that is it can be recalled by stimulating the individual and enkindling in him the spirit of enquiry and love for discovery.

Knowledge, according to him is a part of the soul itself and it is always with the soul, which during the prenatal existence learned all that with which it is familiar in this world. There are, he said, three sources of knowledge: (1) Knowledge obtained through senses; (2) knowledge gained through opinion, and (3) knowledge which is inborn or innate. The knowledge that is derived through senses is not true. The knowledge gathered from opinions may be useful in certain situations, but this knowledge too is not real. The real knowledge is innate, which is reliable. All mathematical truths, general concepts, absolute and abstract ideas are true knowledge. Absolute ideas about beauty, justice, goodness are not acquired through experience. They are already in the possession of the mind.

Being an idealist, Plato emphasised the inculcation of higher values, which he called "Goods of the soul" like justice, self-control, magnanimity and temperance. He deemed self-control and courage, as fundamental virtues for the individual and civil life. He believed in a fixed and unalterable system of training for inculcating moral habits in the youth and, therefore, wanted that the environment of children and the morals and manners of the young and of every citizen should be under drastic censorship.

In the light of his philosophy discussed above, we should now examine Plato's thinking on the concept and Aims of Education, Curriculum. Teaching Methods and Administration of Education

Concept and Aims of Education

Education was highly valued by him and he took an "idealistic and intellectualistic view of education", which was for the good of the individual and for the safety of the State. It was "an essential function of the cosmic order"; It leads to the pursuit of integrity, goodness and perfection. By education he meant "that training which is given by suitable habits to the first instincts of Virtue in Children............ which leads you always to hate what you ought to hate, and love what you ought to love, from the beginning of life to the end". Desires and emotions are to be brought under control so that life of pure reason emerges. To him education is an effort on the part of the older generation to pass on to the younger generation all the good habits and wisdom acquired through experience. He considered education as nothing but the process of re-awakening the consciousness.

Since he advocated the supremacy of the State, his fundamental aim of education was to ensure state-unity. He, therefore, wanted an education, which should discourage 'individualism' and develop a team and co-operative spirit, so as to create a feeling of community life. Every citizen, he affirmed, should be trained to subordinate his individual interests for the sake of the State and thus completely dedicate his life to the service of State. He idolised the State as "a personality that possessed within itself all the factors of the body and mind".

Development of Civic Efficiency was his second aim. This, virtue, he said, could be developed by inculcating "the habits of temperance, courage and military skill into the youth". In order that the appetites in the youth may not have an upper hand, he wanted that education should aim at developing 'reasoning power'. Like the Indian ideals of सत्यम्, शिवम्, सुन्दरम् (Satyam, Shivam, Sundaram), Plato wanted education to aim at inculcating love for truth, goodness and beauty.

On the whole he wanted education to produce a 'whole-man' a unified man' — one who enjoys the "harmony' of the body and the mind; the life of habit and the life of reason, the individual interests and the interests of the State. 'Emphatically he proclaimed, "if our citizens are well educated and grow into sensible men, they will easily see their way through all these matters, as well as other matters which count, such, for example, as marriage, the possession of women and the procreation of children. Education must be a substitute for state regimentation and innumerable laws. It must produce self-governing individuals". "True education", he affirmed, "will have the greatest tendency to civilize and humanise men in their relations to one another, and to those who are under their protection." He considered the school as the greatest humanising and socialising agency. Inculcation of morals and manners was the chief purpose of Plato's education.

Educational Curriculum

Plato's greatest lasting contribution was his scheme of studies or curriculum, which more or less was followed in Western countries identically for several centuries. He wishes binary system of education; *viz.*

1. Education for Practical Affairs.
2. Education for Service to the State.

He confined the education for Practical affairs to the artisan and trade classes. Somehow he had disdain for practical arts, which lie considered mean, vulgar and unfit for a gentleman. He prescribed "no specific training in citizenship for industrial class for he thought that the members of this class had no voice in the government of the State; their characteristic virtue is obedience, technically temperance — to know their place and keep it". He refers to the workers as "those whose natural talents were defective from the first and whose souls have been grievously marred and enervated by their life of drudgery".

Education for service to the State was a sort of liberal education, developing in the learner the ideal perfection of citizenship and equipping him for service to the State. In his liberal education. Plato wanted the development of two types of virtues — fundamental and rational At first the child should develop moral attitudes and habits. For this he regarded discipline and music as the appropriate means. In the old age he recommended the formation of habits by regimentation In the *Laws* he said. "The great principle of all is that no one of either sex should be without a commander........ but in war and peace he should look to and follow his leader."

While in the *Republic*, his education is resuicted to the guardian class, in the *Laws* he wants it to be universal and compulsory, Outlining his system of education m conformity with the biological development of man, he has given the appropriate curriculum for different stages.

During Infancy, that is for the first 2 years, the child was to be properly nourished and saved front pain and wrong pleasure. In the nursery age of 3-6 years, the children were to be given play, fables and fairy tales and simple recreations. Tales, however, should be models of virtuous thoughts.

At the elementary school stage, the boys and girls of 6-13 years were to be housed in separate state dormitories and Plato keeping in view the basic principles of child activities wanted them to be taught music, play, religion, morals, mathematics and gymnastics so as to bring the necessary rhythm, melody and control in the behaviour of children. Musical education, he believed, produces harmony and grace in the individual:

The middle school stage or the period for 13 to 16 years was to be devoted to the learning of music, religious hymns, poetry and arithmetic. It was followed by four years (from 16-20) of gymnastic period, when special attention was to be given to formal gymnastics and military training. There was to be no stress on intellectual training during these years.

Plato recommended higher training at the age of 20 for the most promising young men and women, who should be selected through diagnostic tests for a 10-year course in scientific studies to enable them to see the inter-relationship of facts, do correlated thinking of physical sciences and thus learn these sciences schematically. He says, "The sciences which they learned without any order in their early education will now be brought together and they will be able to see the natural relationship of these to one another and to the True Being." Such people were to become the guardians and rulers of the State and were required to have, "Philosophy and spirit and swiftness and strength." In higher education those persons were to be accepted who were "the bravest; the fairest, having noble and generous tempers, good memory, quickness to leans truth, justice, courage and temperance"

Teaching Methods

In his Academy Plato himself taught mathematics and philosophy by means of correlated lectures and dialogues. His was a method of free self questioning leading to intellectual curiosity. The children should be encouraged to elicit and clarify their own questions. They are to think for themselves and following the line of argument should evolve the truth. If the children make errors because they are yet immature there should be more persistent questioning. His doctrine of "Reminiscence" is in keeping with the motivation provided to pupils to ask the questions themselves and to clear their misgivings and doubts. He did not believe in compulsion as he said, "knowledge which is acquired under compulsion obtains no hold on the mind."

Education of Women

Although he remained a bachelor throughout his life, he conceded that though not so strong the females have fundamentally the same nature as the males. He, therefore, favoured their entry to all the offices and work of the State. He says, "all pursuits of men are the pursuits of women also", and wanted both men and women to be taught music, dancing, gymnastics, military exercises, housemanship and the art of war.

Administration of Education

Believing in the principle of the division of labour, Plato divided the citizens of a State into three classes; *viz.* (1) industrial or artisan class, (2) military class; and (3) governing or philosopher or ruler class. For each of these classes he wanted different forms of training. In the *Republic*, however, he has discussed the education of the philosopher (or governor or ruler) and the soldier (military class) but not of industrial and artisan class, for whom probably he wanted Vocational training only'.

Provision of education, he averred, is the primary duty of the State. All the children should be in the public schools, conducted and controlled by the State and must be educated alike, no one being allowed to have his own will apart from that of the community.

A superintendent of education should be elected by the magistrates from among the ablest citizens of the State. He should be over 50 years old and hold the office for 5 years. In the discharge of his duties, the superintendent be assisted by the director of music, director of gymnastics and other assistants and superintendents for organising contests.

2

Jean Jacques Rousseau

(1712 TO 1778)

The 18th century is called the age of faith, hope and reason. It was humanitarian age which attempted to abolish slavery, to reform prisons, to alleviate the miseries of the peasant, to educate the blind and deaf and to deal with children kindly and intelligently. In the political sphere the democratic trends were ushering in. In literature the century turned from classicism to romanticism. In religion there was the spread of Pietism.

All this had influence on education. The schools, wherever they existed, were narrow in then content, formal in methods and harsh in discipline. The educators of the tune therefore, developed new interest in health and physical education, in science and the study of Nature, in the use of sense and the effort to teach pupils to think for themselves, and in the practical arts. Rousseau was one of the prophets of this new education.

His Life

In '*Confessions*' Rousseau has told his autobiography with the frankness. He was born in Geneva. In this city there prevailed moral life, purity of domestic relatins, simplicity of social order and freedom Government, in share contrast to life at Paris where there was luxury, artificiality and immorality. Rousseau's mother died at his birth and this was his first misfortune. Naturally he grew to be a sensitive and neurotic child. His father also was unfit to look after him. At the age of ten he was committed to the care of this uncle. who proved as his father. Rousseau's extraordinary talents, therefore, received no systematic cultivation for 2 years. He was sent to a tutor to learn Latin and other subject. Some Drawing and Geometry was taught to him but he was taught no vocation to earn his livelihood m the later life. His only passion at the early age was the reading of romances.

At the age of 12 he was apprenticed to a trade, where according to him he learnt more of deceit, idleness and dishonesty than he did craftsmanship. For a long time he remained a vagabond. This, of course, created in him love for, and knowledge of Nature. A full meal, a bottle of wine and the hospitality of a priest led his conversion to a different religion and that shaped the life of Rousseau for some years.

In 1741 he became a tutor to the two sons of a Provost but he could not pull on account of his irritable temper. This experience of teaching, however, gave him permanent interest in education.

His family life was as unsettled as his childhood and youth. It was marked by hardship and sometimes by unseemly deeds. As the secretary to a lady he stole a ribbon, and placed the blame on an innocent servant girl, who lost her job. At 32 he married an innocent servant girl, by whom he had 5 children. Unfortunately all these were sent to the orphanage one by one even against the tearful protest of the mother.

After attempting, however, many occupations like private tutor, music teacher, composer, secretary and dramatist, it was at the age of 38 that he became a successful writer. In 1778 he died in Paris. In spite of his many faults and his being the innocent victim of great misfortunes he propounded a theory of education which is now termed as Naturalism.

As a Writer

The first treatise on education was his Project for the Education of M. de Sainte Marie" written in 1740 for the two sons of the Provost whom he taught. In this treatise he laid down the aim of education for a child as "to form Ins heart, his judgement and his mind". This work anticipated "Emile' — an educational treatise of 500 pages.

In 1750 he wrote a "Discourse on the Sciences and Arts". This was an answer to a question: has the restoration of sciences contributed to purify or corrupt man? Rousseau's answer was negative. In this book he propounded his doctrine of "Natural State".

It was maintained that culture and learning had made men luxurious and effeminate. Men had neglected their duties as citizens and parents. He believed that "a thatched roof covered Free men; under marble and gold dwells slavery." He argued that the days of poverty, simplicity and ignorance were the days of strength, happiness and innocence. His emphasis was on moral and virtuous life.

In his second book "Discourse on the origin of unequality among men", published in 1755, he concluded that in a state of Nature men were more equal than they were under civilization. Civilization created a sense of possession and that in turn created inequality, which is a positive evil. He wanted, therefore, to return to a State of Nature.

After these Discourses, Rousseau remained busy from 1750 to 1762 in writing work of educational interest — "Discourse of Political Economy, the New Heloise, the Social Contract, the Emile and the Considerations on the Government of Poland". Of all these, 'Emile' is his main treatise on education. In the Discourse of Political Economy, Rousseau gives, besides other things, his views on national and public education. The New Heloise refers to family education but propounds new ideas, which are not found in Emile.

In his most famous book — 'Social Contract' he says that Government is the result of a contract among the people by which sonic are given delegated power to rule, while the remainder of the people give to the Government mere sendee. Government formed by agreement can be dissolved when the parties no longer agree Conception of the "Natural State" is modified in the Social Contract, His ideal is no longer the life of the savage but the life and society organized under the rule of the people. In this state the simple tastes and wants of the masses dominate. Aristocracy with its ill-gained wealth, leisure-time and selfish indulgence is given no importance. Such a society can devote itself to the development of an ideal life. His "Considerations on the Government of Poland" shows an application of his principles of national education.

His Philosophy

Three influences worked in shaping his general philosophy *viz.*, the state of time, varied experience of his life and his emotional Nature. His works give insight into his political, social and educational philosophy. The key mole of his philosophy was to have a 'State of Naturey 'Natural Man' and 'Natural Civilizations "Civilized

Man" says Rousseau "is born, lives and dies in a state of slavery. At his birth he is stitched in swaddling clothes; at his death he is nailed in his coffin and as long as he preserves the human form he is fettered by our institutions. Leave him alone". Rousseau wanted men to be free from the bondage of society by educating them not for citizenship but for manhood. He believed that civilization, the arts and all human institutions had pernicious effect. According to him the source of all social evils is to be found in the restless curiosity of which of the sciences and arts are the final products. Man, he believed, would have been happier if he had been allowed to remain in his primitive stage as a creature of feeling. Man had brought misery to him by his own inventions. Rousseau, therefore, stated that these inventions should be scrapped off and the man would become happy.

Rousseau's philosophy is designated as 'Naturalism'. He contended that all the ills and miseries of civilization are due to a departure horn a State of Nature. "Everything is good as it corner from the hands of the Author of Nature; but everything degenerates m the hands of mail declared Rousseau in the opening sentence of 'Emile' which appeared in 1762. Return to Nature, therefore, was his method to cure the world of troubles. Life according to Nature was genuine. It recognised the worth of the individual on his own merits. It was free from the trammels of usage tradition and tyranny.

By Natural state and Natural man he did not want the primitive social order and the savage man. He wanted natural civilization and a fully developed man living in the whirl of social life without being carried away by the passion and prejudices of society. Reason, he said, should be the guiding principle in producing both the Natural civilization and Natural man. His ideal of the 'State of Nature' was "a simple farming community or state without evils" which he ascribed to large cities, corrupt rulers, social classes and luxury."

Tradition believed that human Nature was evil and must be changed or disciplined. Rousseau said that human Nature is good and should be allowed a free development. Education, therefore, must be in ham tony with original and unspoiled human Nature. By Nature here Rousseau meant native instincts, tendencies and capacities. He held that learning takes place best when child is free to develop and grow according to his natural impulses. He was convinced that child's original nature is good and pure. But since the child is immature and unable to care for himself, education is necessary The function of education is to preserve the child's goodness and purity without stain from the world. Conditions should be created that the child may grow and mature. Human restraints and discipline should be discarded. Rousseau was a hater of imposed authority His appeal is always to Nature as against civilization and society. He was a lover of Nature, mountains and streams, of sunrise and sun-set, of solitude and the country life. Such setting, said he, should be provided that the child can engage in those activities which interest him. His Naturalism holds that the best learning comes from dealing with Natural objects, with manual arts and with persons in a natural way. Learning is hampered by too great insistence on mathematics, language and books. The catch words of Naturalism are freedom, growth, interest and activity. How well-known are these to the modern progressive education.

Rousseau glorified the wholesome development of all the natural powers of the individual. If the individual is nurtured properly so that his physical, emotional, moral, mental capacities are allowed to develop naturally and at the proper time, the cause of education and the society will be best served. He looked to the individual rather than to the society to find the ultimate aims of education.

His Meaning of Nature

Society for him, was artificial and not natural. In 'Emile' he described and education based, not on the social aspect and on the meaningless traditions of the school, but on the knowledge of true nature of man. Every man has laws of this own nature. Education must be guided by those laws. A natural education must be given to man. It does not mean on education. It signifies simply a non-social education. This, in the opinion of Rousseau, was a preventive education. Such education does not prepare for life, but it prepares against the social conditions which man has to confront in later life. From this it should not be understood that Rousseau wanted to create un-social creatures. His objective was to save the man from the evil influences of society.

The second meaning given to Mature' is the instinctive judgement, primitive emotions, natural instincts or innate tendencies. These, according to Rousseau, are more reliable basis for action than the experience gained from the society. There should, therefore, be spontaneous development of these.

The third meaning attached by Rousseau to the term 'nature' is positive. One who is brought up in the natural environments automatically becomes a rational being. He acts according to the voice of his conscience and one "who obeys Ins conscience is following nature."

Nature, the Chief Teacher

Rousseau said that man is educated by three things — Nature, Men and Things. "The internal development of our organs and faculties is the education of nature; the use we are taught to make of that development is the education given its by men, and the acquisition made by our own experience on the objects that surround us, consists our education from things."

By 'nature' Rousseau meant natural tendencies unchanged by habit or prejudices He advocated natural interest. The body senses, intellect and heart display each one in turn from birth to manhood, then own special interest. When these appear, education must conform with them. There are, said Rousseau, sharply defined stages in human development. Each one of these stages is marked by its own predominant and unmistakable interest which 'nature' herself has created. For example, at the age of 12 or 13 rational interests appear. At the age of 15 or 16 the sex urge comes up and is followed by many social interests. The special interest, urge or demand of 'nature' at each and every stage of human development is the guide the next stage but only perfect the child's development at the stage he has reached.

His Methods of Education

The traditional system of education aimed to remark the 'nature' of the child by forcing upon him the traditional way of thinking, of doing and even of emotional reaction. Natural instincts and interests of the child were given no consideration. Human senses had no place as the basis for knowledge or instruction. Effort was made to mould the child into the artificial forms of conduct, satisfactory to the judgement of the adult. The mind was considered as a bundle of faculties. These faculties were deemed to have no necessary connection with each other. Each faculty was developed separately by teaching certain subjects. For instance, the faculty of reasoning was developed by mathematics, logic and languages. Memory was developed through learning the material for which the child had no inherent interest.

From the sociological point of view the child was considered a miniature adult. His training, therefore, was conducted on such pattern. He was expected to speak, think and act as a miniature adult. He was taught the same subjects as the adult. Languages and formal grammar were taught to him and these he learnt through sheer effort of memory.

Rousseau revolted against this entire conception of education. Education, he believed, is a natural not an artificial process. "It is a development from within, not an accretion from without." This, he said, could be acquired by exploiting the natural instincts and interests rather than by external force. He wanted the child to learn that winch is not irksome, and not foisted on him against his will. To him education was a continuous process — a process lasting throughout life, or at least from birth to adulthood. It is not mere acquisition of information, but the expansion of natural powers it is life itself and not a preparation for uncertain future.

Traditionally, the aim of education was held to be 'social' 'vocational' or 'spiritual' preparation. For Rousseau the aim of education was "the attainment of fullest natural growth of the individual." The teacher, he said can train the man or the citizen; he cannot train both. Natural man is greater than the citizen. He is the unit, and the citizen but the fraction. He, therefore, wanted the teacher to form 'natural men'. He wanted the men first before they were lawyers soldiers or divine. They should be educated first for manhood and then for citizenship. A person who had attained manhood could be sure of success in any profession. His natural men were those whose natural virtues had not been influenced by traditional and social institutions. On the other hand their natural virtues were so developed that they were able to adapt themselves to the changing environments. This, he believed, could be achieved through education and through the guidance of the teacher. Education, to Rousseau, was a process of guidance by the teacher rather than instruction by him. The teacher's primary duty was to make the pupil wish to learn by exploiting his innate dispositions.

He was emphatic in saying that' education was a process of development into an enjoyable, rational, harmoniously balanced, useful and hence natural life. He condemned the artificial, harsh, unsympathetic methods of education, which repressed all natural inclination. Simple and direct methods of instruction were advocated by him. Laying a special emphasis on 'object teaching', he remarked, "let the senses always be the guides" let there be no books but the world and no other instruction than facts. The child who reads does not think — he merely reads; he is not receiving instruction, but learning words," Rousseau wanted that Geography should be learnt in the woods and the fields, by the observation of the position of the sun and the earth, by the study of the stream, the rain and the changes of the temperature. He would have astronomy learnt by the study of heavenly bodies and botany by the study of plants. Similarly facts and principles of physics and chemistry by observation and experimentation. Mathematics could be learnt in connection with these subjects and the economic relation. It was history alone which could be learnt through, reading. All subjects he said, were to begin at home He said that only that should be attempted winch car be understood. Only that which can be mastered should taught. His advice was that "in general, never substitute the sign for the thing itself save when it is impossible to snow the thing, for the signs absorb the attention of the child and makes turn forget the thing represented." All these precepts of Rousseau are being increasingly recognized and realized in modern education winch lays the greatest stress on concrete teaching.

He objected to verbalism in education words, words, words nothing but words. They were being memorised but not understood Child, he believed, should be taught by experience and not by verbal lesson; by his own reason when it develops and not by the reasoning of adults. Memory and reason develop together. The former depends upon the latter. The child may learn words mechanically, but it is only through judgement that he understands ideas and relations. Rousseau found that all that was foreign to the minds of the children, was being taught to them. Books suited to children hardly existed. Instruction was a tiresome task both for children and for teacher. It was Rousseau who advocated the playway method. In every play he saw the opportunity of giving the child some instruction or the other. For example in jumping, climbing, balancing making a swing the children learnt how to judge and measure distances. Said Rousseau, that to 'Emile', "work or play are all one to him, his games are his work; he knows no difference." He said that children could learn drawing because they were great imitators. His ideal was to have no masters but 'nature' and no models but objects.

'Know childhood', was his first precept. Ignorance of child nature is the root of educational errors. The tutor should study the nature of his pupil. Each mind has a form of its own; but the traits of the child's mind can be learnt only by observation as they develop. A wise education proceeds by observing the child and adapting its measures to his individual capacities and needs.

In this way criticising the practices and methods of education prevalent in his day, he propounded naturalistic principles and applied them to an imaginary pupil named 'Emile' from the moment of his birth to his manhood. This work of 500 pages is divided into five pans, four of which deal with Emile's education in infancy, childhood, boyhood and youth. The fifth part deals with the training of Sophie', — a girl who has to become the ideal wife of 'Emile'.

Application of the Above Stated Principles in 'Emile'

The principles stated above have been included in the plan of education for Emile. Since the educator has to begin by the study of the child he must take into account four factors:

1. *The generic character of mankind i.e.* those characters wind. are variously manifested in the dispositions or inclinations.

2. *Different characteristics of sexes.* It is his first principle of natural education as Rousseau understands if that sex should be taken into account in the upbringing of boys and girls. According to him the nature of the two sexes is fundamentally different from the very beginning. That makes necessary the corresponding difference in their education. For this reason he would have the boy educated to be a complete human being with world-wide interest, and the girl to be trained exclusively for wifehood and motherhood.

3. *Difference of individuality.* Each mind has a form of its own. It must, therefore, be directed accordingly. Individuality, he pointed out, raises many problems "one has to be flattered, another has to be repressed. One man is made to carry human knowledge to its furthest point, another may find the ability to read a dangerous power."

4. *Differences of age.* Each age and condition of life has a perfection and maturity of his own.

The answer to all the problems arising out of these factors has been given in "Emile" and 'New Helois.' In Emile' the education of the boy is the social care of the tutor, who devotes the best part of his life to the task. The tutor must exercise perfect control of all the circumstances likely to determine his mind and character. In the 'New Helots' he has two boys and one girl growing up in the well regulated liberty of an household under the eyes of enlightened parents, who take care not to interfere with the lessons of experience. Rousseau believed that home education is the best education. Mother is the proper nurse and father is the best teacher. The family in fact stands midway between nature and society. It is there, better than anywhere, that the child can develop his individual powers with the minimum of restraint and yet be prepared for his place in the great world of men.

Believing that every age has a special character of its own, Rousseau divides the time of pupil age into four periods in 'Emile' and defined their characteristic features in order to prescribe the appropriate education for each. While he distinguishes the different phases of growth he assumes two things; One, that there is a certain correspondence between the growth of individual and the history of the race. Two, that childhood is a time of mental passivity from which the child gradually transforms into mental activity of manhood. This transformation takes place by a successive maturing of facilities. His educational scheme, based upon the principles of age grouping, is as follows.

Period of Infancy

It is a period from birth to the age of five. The child during these years is to all intents and purposes an animal. He is in a state of undifferentiated feeling. He is scarcely more conscious of himself than in the prenatal life. Education begins at birth with the physical and social reactions caused by the child's bodily activity. The main rule for the educator, at this stage, is not to spoil the lessons of experience by too much neglect or too much indulgence. Let him not be subdued. Let him not be pampered. In order to acquire the elementary arts or eating, speaking and walking in these years the child requires unconscious imitation and personal effort.

Rousseau did not want any restrictions on the child regarding clothing and movement. He wanted him to follow his natural inclination, and desires. Let him creep about to get exercise. His body must be hardened to bear all seasons, hunger, thirst and fatigue. For example bathe him at first in the warm but gradually in cooler water until at last it may be quite cold. 'Emile' must live an active, vigorous, out-door life both to develop his body and to train his senses while he acquires a knowledge of natural objects and forces. The young child should be gradually accustomed to strange sights and noises, so that he may not be frightened by masks, firearms, and ugly annuals. His tears should not become commands If he cries because of discomfort or pain, he should be relieved, but without being caressed or rocked to sleep. His play-things should be very simple such as branches with limits and flowers and no expensive toys.

Since the child cannot bare the conception of right and wrong, punishment for any of his acts should be avoided. He should be allowed to wander freely on the country-side and fake part in sports games and exercise. Rousseau laid great stress on physical strength as he believed that "the weaker the body, die more is commands; the stronger it is, the better obeys. All the sensual passions find lodgment in effeminate bodies. All wickedness conics front weakness. A child is bad only because he is weak, make him strong and he will be good. He who can do everything does nothing bad."

Regarding Ins intellectual and moral development, not much attention is to be paid. His vocabulary should be limited. Only those ideas should be given to him about which he can think and understand. He should hear only simple, well articulated words and cheerful songs. This is chiefly a period of physical education, freedom and activity.

Childhood

The period remains up to the age of 12 years. It is the most critical period of human life. The child's mind is dominated by the senses. The period may aptly be called the period of sense education. The child lacks any proper power of reasoning. He cannot understand right and wrong. No commands, therefore, should be given to him. Necessity must be his teacher. Let him learn by experience and the results of his own conduct. If the child breaks something he must remain without it. If he tells a lie, he would not be believed. If he falls he will be hurt and in future he will be more careful Punishment must never be inflicted on him, but should always come to him as the natural consequence of his own imprudence. If 'Emile' breaks a window pane, let him suffer the resulting inconvenience or it is better for him to have a cold than to be a fool.

Early education should chiefly be negative. It should consist, '"not in the teaching of virtue or of truth, but in the preservation of heart from vice and the mind from error." The boy at this stage is as yet too immature to understand moral facts. No attempt should be made to teach morality, except when can it be reduced to physical terms, for example, by comparing anger with fear. The child learns the moral by example rather than by precept, Acts of charity and goodness performed in his presence will make him charitable and kind. Nothing at all should be done towards moulding or forcing his mind. Childhood is for its own sake. "Nature desires that children should be children before they are men." That's why Rousseau wants 'Emile' to be brought up in the country, away from the evils and vices of the city.

Rousseau recommends different methods of teaching them. He says that it is cam to teach them ordinary school subjects. Language, geography history etc., all emply an understanding of the facts of life beyond the comprehension of the boy. If they are taught they will be learnt only as empty word and thus pervert the mind by semblance of knowledge. The only direct education appropriate at tins stage is the training of mind through physical activities. "'Exercise the body, the organs, the senses and powers, but keep the soul lying fallow as long as you can." To him this is the stage for sense training. Senses are the instruments of intellect. These can be trained by intimate contact with the forces and phenomena of nature. "The senses are the first faculty to take form and attain perfection, and consequently should be the first to be cultivated. These are the basis of thought and reason. Feet, hands and eyes are our first teachers. They must not be substituted by books. On the other hand they must be developed by appropriate exercises. Training of senses calls for more than the mere use of them. It means learning to judge, foresee and reason through them. Sight, for example, is perfected by exercises in the measurement and estimation of distance, drawing from actual objects, practical geometry and bargains. To spring from one end of the hall to the other, to estimate the bound of the ball still in the air and to send it back with a strong and steady hand, trams both the limbs and the senses. All the lemming must come by play-way. There should he no compulsion except that of personal desire. Some critics might point out that in this way the early years of the child will be wasted in doing nothing, but Rousseau replies. "Is it nothing to be happy? — to jump, play, run, all day long?"

Some general ideas, however, may be taught to the child. One of these it the idea about property. This can be done in a garden where he should have a plot to himself to plant some beans. He will have the idea of mine and thine and will assimilate more language before he can have a complete idea of property. Geometry, drawing and music should also be taught through experience, projects and active doing. Geometry can be taught not by demonstration but by drawing figures and by computing and measuring them. He should learn drawing by drawing natural objects. Music may be learnt by rote-singing.

Instruction at this age must conform with the child's ability. He should not be exhausted mentally. "Not to gain time but to loose it" for the sake of happy childhood is his main rule. There is no need far the child to learn anything by heart. "What is the significance of imprinting on their minds a catalogue of signs which to them represent nothing?" At the end of this period his senses will be fully developed and he would be ready for reasoning. He had few ideas but they are precise, because they have come from experience and from the book of nature. "He pursues no formula, is influenced by no authority but acts and speaks from his own judgement.

The age of Pre-adolescence

This period is covered from the age of 12 to the age of 15. It is a period of intellectual education. The boy is on the verge of adult life. He gains in physical strength and with it intellect also makes its appearance. Reason and self consciousness have also appeared. It is, therefore, the time for work, instruction and enquiry. It is the time for developing intellect. So far necessity has been the guide, now utility should determine the course. In these transition years, curiosity "develops and creates in the boy an urge for knowledge. Rousseau rejected, "from our primary studies those branches of nature for which man has not a natural taste and limited us to those which instinct leads us to pursue." This principle is very widely accepted to-day.

This period is so short that Rousseau advises that it should be used very wisely. In the previous period losing time was, virtue. It is not so now. Hie curriculum, therefore, should be built around curiosity and useful activities, which are the only real motives of learning. 'Emile' is introduced to studies that reveal nature, astronomy, science and the arts and crafts He should deal with these problems on his own resources independent of the authority or advice of other people. Rousseau gives an example of how to begin the study of science. For this, there are mo starting points; one from the boy's interest m the world around him (geography), the other from his interest in the sun (astronomy), the two converging later towards the underlying principles of physics. The object is not to give him knowledge but the taste and the capacity for acquiring it, and the method should be that of personal discovery "He is not to learn science, he is to find it out for himself." He should learn by his own efforts through the observation of nature. This is Ins theory of learning by doing. While teaching him geography Rousseau does not want the child to be shown the globes and maps, but the earth, the sky, the setting and the rising of the sun. Rousseau thinks that the study of books and language is harmful to the child's nature. He substitutes play, sports, games and the manual arts and the arts of developing sense experience. The only book which he recommends is 'Robinson Crusoe', a study of 'life according to nature". He emphasises the learning of manual and industrial arts partly to make the boy independent of any change of fortune and partly to overcome the prejudices held against the manual work. It would show the boy how men depend upon each other. Rousseau said that the boy must be taken from one workshop to another and he must try his hand at every trade. In this way Rousseau wanted to teach him industrial exchange, banking and transportation. Learning of trade, said Rousseau, would also teach the boy mental discipline. By including the craft in the scheme of studies we have its reflection in the basic education of Gandhiji.

At the conclusion of this period Emile is industrious, temperate, patient, firm and full of courage. He has little knowledge but what he has is really his own; he knows "nothing by halves".

This period in fact should prepare the way for the next period, which would be concerned with moral and social conduct and religion. Necessity, utility and morality form the 3 successive spirals of human development. In the previous period the child studied what was necessary. In this period, he studies what is useful. In the next period the emphasis would be on morality and virtue.

Adolescence

The period of adolescence extends from the age of 15 to the time of marriage, say about 25. Until 15 Emile's body, senses and brain were formed. Now the training of heart should receive attention, because body, senses, mind and heart compose the whole man. So far the boy was an individual, working for self perfection and self development. Now he has to be social and adapt himself to the conduct and interests of others. He must be loving and compassionate. He should love all mankind. He should have pity for the afflicted ones. These are the virtues to be inculcated and can be acquired by observing the sufferings of the poor, the sick and the social out-castes.

At this stage the youth undergoes a new birth on account of the appearance of sex impulse. Soul is now added to the intellect and sense, Beauty, goodness and truth acquire a personal value. Conscience rules life. Virtue is possible. Rousseau, therefore, wants the real education to begin (Is it not just the time when ordinary system of education ends?).

The first lesson that the youth has to learn at this stage is the control of the passions, now surging up in the soul. For this he should have moral and religious education. He must follow natural religion, which teaches him the existence of God, soul, rewards and punishments. Feeling and conscience tells him right and wrong and they never deceive him. One who obeys them, will never commit any wrong. Questions of religion and morality are answered by conscience as well as by the book of nature. It is only through nature that one can know God and love him. 'Emile' must be told by the tutor the dangers of the sex. Information rather than ignorance would help him to restrain. Besides protecting him from harmful companions and influences he must be kept busy in hard work. If dignity of marriage is impressed upon him he will certainly control his sex. A taste for literature will counteract the tendency of his brain becoming a devils' workshop.

The study of society, politics, economics, history and religion are the appropriate studies for the youth to understand complex social relationship. He should study men as individuals and their institutional relationships. History would help him to judge character. If he wants to be a man he must know the world, To know the world he must travel through neighbouring countries and study then language, institutions and their Governments Similarly the development of a moral view, spiritual aspirations and aesthetic tastes is important. The youth can very well understand these things now through the study of language, philosophy psychology, religion and other arts.

Unlike his childhood the education of 'Emile' has now to be positive and not negative. He is now not only to shun the evil as previously, but he has to do the good as well. In the earlier period has had to learn everything by his own experience. Now he can benefit from the experience of others. It is after his stage that he meets an ideal woman and marries her.

Education of Sophy

At the end of 'Emile' Rousseau wants the hero of his educational romance to marry Sophy, the girl worthy to he married to Ins paragon From the earlier writings of Rousseau we learn that he gave women a higher place than men. He maintained that women were the makers of men. They were, "the chaste" guardians of our morals and the sweet security for our peace." They were born to govern the men Bur his own unfortunate experiences with women changed his views. He came to believe that men and women are not and ought not to be constituted alike in character and temperament. Therefore they ought not to have the same education. The education of a woman, he wanted, to be relative to man because he believed that "woman is made specially to please man." She has to be constrained and taught docility. She must be soft and sweet and learn, to suffer and to bear the wrongs of her husband without complaint. Towards man the duty of woman is, "to train him in childhood, to tend him in manhood, and to counsel him throughout his life."

While for a boy he laid down naturalistic individual education, for a girl he prescribed passive and repressive framing. He allows no individuality to woman and considers has as simply supplementary to the nature of man. Women, in his opinion, should be given physical training to develop her physical charms and to produce healthy children. In order to satisfy their instinct of pleasing others through dress, women should be taught sewing, embroidery and lace work They should also be taught singing, dancing and other accomplishments Ethics and religion must be taught but no philosophy science or art Rousseau wanted the girl to be taught religion, which should he very simple. She should not be asked to learn anything by heart, not even her prayers. With a few doctrines and fewer observances she should believe that, "there is a judge of human faith, that we are all His children, that He bids us all to be just. He bids us love one another. He bids us be kindly and merciful. He bids us keep our word with all men, with out enemies and His; we must know that the apparent happiness of this world is naught; and that there is another life to come in which this Supreme Being will be the rewarder of the just and the judge of the unjust."

Compared with the bey the girl has to be kept under more restraints and should he taught to he obedient and industrious. Although Rousseau considered women mentally inferior to men and incapable of abstract reasoning, yet he would have Sophy, taught, reading, writing and ciphering when she felt a need for them. All her studies, he wanted, should be practical, intellectual interests, he believed, destroy her nature. He said, "The search for abstract and speculative truths, for principles and actions in science, for all that tends to wide generalization, is beyond a woman's grasp." Again he said, "I would a hundred tunes prefer a simple girl, rudely brought up, to a girl of learning and who would come to establish in my house a literary tribunal of which she should make herself the president. A woman of wit is the scourge of her husband, her children, her friends....... of everybody."

The ideal natural woman is modest, gentle, patient, submissive, sensitive to rebukes, amiable, chaste and charitable in her thoughts and words. In expressing the views on women and their education Rousseau, somehow, does not show a progressive outlook. Judged from the standard of 'equality of opportunity irrespective of sex' the view is one-sided and narrow. Is it not an oriental conception of women, when he says — "the man should be strong and active; the woman should be weak and passive. A man seeks to serve, a woman seeks to please; the one needs knowledge, the other taste."

Criticism of Emile

'Emile' was severely criticised by the Parliament of Paris. The book was ordered to be publicly burnt. Order for the arrest of the author was issued and he had to fly away from France to Switzerland. The Archbishop of Pans forbade the reading of Trade and condemned if as a hooky 'Containing an abominable doctrine, ready to subvert natural law and to destroy the foundations of the Christian religion..... tending to trouble the peace of states, to cause subjects to revolts against their sovereigns, as containing a large number of prepositions false, scandalous, full of hate against the church..... derogatory to the respect of holy scripture..... erroneous, impious, blasphemous and heretical."

It was believed that in 'Emile' the individual became the fundamental and the society was subordinated It was doubted how could education take place m a social vacuum. In bringing up of his model child, he neglected parents, brothers and sisters and other young companions.

Rousseau believed that the states exist for the individuals and not the individuals for the state. The individuals do not exist for democracy; democracy exists for the individual, for the freedom of man and growth of individuality. This view of Rousseau, contrary to the present view of democracy, was also not looked with favour by politicians and statesmen.

As regards the positive criticism 'Emile' was accounted a work of great richness, power and underlying wisdom. Each of its defect is more than balanced by a corresponding merit. It is a protest against the traditional education, which was psychologically unsound, practically unreal and socially and philosophically unprogressive. It was a protest against the education which ignored the child and was bookish. It brought an era of educational reform not only in psychology and methods of instruction but also in the movement to reform society by means of education.

It was a book which had great effect on thought and action of education in the 18th century. It was immediately translated into several languages. It aroused a deep interest in the problems of childhood and youth. In the words of William Boyd, "Society women began to nurse their own babies, fathers and mothers attempted to bring up their children as Emiles and Sophies, some more enthusiastic than the rest kept diaries m which they recorded their observations of their little ones, many of the nobles installed workshops in then homes to give their sons a training in some craft, writers produced a new literature for the young........... There was general agreement that no form of education could be regarded as satisfactory winch did not take account of the nature of the child." It was increasingly realised that new schemes to improve the education were most essential. Speaking of Emile Lord Morley said that it was, "one of the seminal books in history of literature, and of such books the worth resides less in the parts than in the whole it touched the deeper dungs things of character. It filled parents with a sense of dignity and moment of their task. It cleared the accumulation of clogging prejudices and obscure inveterate usage. If admitted floods of light and air into the tightly dosed nurseries and school rooms. It effected the substitution of growth for mechanism. It was the charter of youthful deliverance.

His Influence on Educational Thought and Practice

In the words of R.H. Quick, "Rousseau did in the world of ideas what the French Revolutionists afterwards did in the world of politics, he made a clean sweep and endeavoured to start afresh." Rousseau wanted not reform but revolution in the field of education. He has influenced a great many educators, in his teachings are found the educational developments of the 19th and 20th centuries. He denounced the old and showed the new. This became the inspiration to all educational reformers of the future, who reduced Ins theories in the practical procedure.

Sociological Emphasis : The greatest contribution of Rousseau was his emphasis that education should prepare the individual to live in a society. Thus he laid the foundation for the sociological tendency in modem education. In his individualism, he emphasized the idea of a social education of a new type. This can be seen by his inclusion of manual art in his scheme of studies and in his emphasis on moral and emotional education as against the intellectual. He wanted everyone to contribute by his own labour to his own support, should be bound by sympathy to all his fellow men and by benevolence to all who needed his aid. Present-day emphasis upon vocational education and moral instruction find their root in Emile.

Psychological Tendency. Rousseau was the forerunner of modern psychology because he emphasised the importance of (1) Individual differences; (2) Psychology of growth; (3) Growth of education out of native interests and curiosity; (4) Education by judgement and reason rather than by memory.

Before Rousseau there was emphasis on curriculum. It is under his influence that education became paedo-centric in post-Rousseau times. For Emile there is no fixed curriculum.

He has to learn by activity and experience. Curriculum-centric education was replaced by child-centric education.

Treat your pupil according to his age. This is the most practical suggestion of Rousseau. He had shown the characteristic differences at the various stages in child's life and laid down that a child can reach maturity or perfection only if appropriate activities are provided at each stage. He did not warn any fixed method of thinking feeling and acting to be forced upon the child. By laying 'curiosity' and 'interest' as the motives of learning he anticipated Herbart in formulating his steps for lessons. It is due to Rousseau that the importance of physical activities and sense training in the earlier period of life as the foundation for its later growth and learning are being increasingly recognised.

Discovery and recognition of childhood traits: It was Rousseau who emancipated the child from trammels of society and mediaeval restraint. Be was the first person to give the child his rightful place. Emile was called the charter of youthful deliverance. Be said, "Love childhood, indulge its sports, its pleasure, its delightful instinct. Why rob these innocents (children) of the joys which pass so quickly...............? Why fill with bitterness the fleeting days of early childhood, days winch will no more return for them........? Fathers, can you tell when death will call your children to Him? Do not lay up sorrow for yourselves by robbing them of the short span which nature has allotted to them. As soon as they are aware of the job of life, let them rejoice in it, so that whenever God calls them they may not die without having tasted the joy of life." Rousseau believed in the innate goodness of the child. Therefore he emphasized sympathy with childhood as the qualification for all educational work. This theory by Rousseau was made practice by Pestalozzi and has come to be recognised as an essential in the educative process. He recognised the importance of child activity For this the modern activists owe their debts to Rousseau. At all times he stressed not the activity of the teacher by the activity of the child. He was the great discoverer of the child and said. "Childhood has ways of seeing, drinking and feeling, peculiar to itself, nothing can be more foolish than to substitute our ways for them."

His emphasis on the concrete: As against verbalism and book learning Rousseau emphasised the value of concrete objects. Learning by doing was his great principle and he included those subjects in the curriculum, which can be learnt by experience in the natural environments. Rousseau's leaching that the educational material should be the facts and phenomena of nature, strongly reinforced the scientific tendency in modern education. 'Object teaching' of Pestalozzi and "Motor expression' of Froebel were inspired by Rousseau and this is what is being stressed in the present-day education.

Anticipated Modern Heuristic Method : Prescribing the method of teaching science, Rousseau said, "Put the problems before him (child) and let him solve them himself. Let him know nothing because you have told him, but because he has learnt for himself. Let him not be taught science, let Mm discover it." This later came to be known as Heuristic method.

Showed the way to the teacher: Rousseau announced the true nature of teacher's profession. He advised them, "study the subject you have to act upon." This is the starting point of 'New Education'. The educator got a fresh conception of his task. Teaching became a new occupation with boundless possibilities and unceasing interest in it. Every teacher became a learner, for he had to study the minds of the young, their way of looking at things, their habits, their difficulties, their likes and dislikes. They studied how children are to be stimulated to exertion, how they are discouraged, and how one mood succeeds another. They tried to gain knowledge of the human mind with the object of influencing it appropriately.

Rousseau was a great revolutionary. Led partly the personal feeling and partly by sympathy for the common people he revolted against the social inequalities of his age. He propounded in place of the old law of reason, the new gospel of faith in nature, "in the common man and in man's ability to work out his own good life. He worked out a new ideal in life, infused a new spirit in society and re-established a basis for religion in man's nature."

Although Rousseau possessed an unusual power of embodying great ideas in words, he had very slight ability to realise them in action. His ideas were never fully put into practice in any single school.

His greatest contribution in the field of education was his educational methods, "by showing the value of motivation, of creating problems, and of utilising the senses and activities of the child" His conceptions of freedom, growth, interest and activity were greatly needed at the time against authoritarianism and absolutism in education. His idea, in brief, was that human happiness and human welfare are the natural rights of every man and not the special privilege of a favoured class. This human happiness, he believed, could be realised by a proper type of social organisation and education. He said that sound education should play the role of developing wholesome individuals in a wholesome society. Education, he averred, must work on both fronts, on the individual and the society.

3

Friedrich August Froebel

(1783—1852)

"Froebel, the pupil of pestalozzi, and a genius like his master, completed the reformer's system; taking the results at which Pestalozzi had arrived..... Froebel developed the ideas involved in them, not by further experience but by deduction from the nature of man, and thus he attained to the conception of true human development and to the requirements of true education."

Friedrich Wilhelm August Froeble was a German and was born on 21st April, 1783. He lost his mother in his childhood. His father, who was not interested in the family, got re-married. With the coming in of step-mother, a maternal uncle of Froebel took pity on him and took him to his village. Since his own childhood was neglected, Froeble spent his life in promoting the happiness of children.

He was admitted to the village school but he did not do well there. At the age of 14 he was apprenticed for two years to a forester. It was hare that his love for nature grew. Without scientific instruction he obtained a profound insight into the uniformity and essential unity of nature's laws. This created in him a longing to study nature's universal laws. For this he joined at the University of Jena, but the poor fellow had to give up University career for lack of funds. For about 4 years he remained on career-wanderings — trying his hands sometimes as a Private Secretary. With all these circumstances still he felt that he was destined to a great task but the nature of the task was not clear to him.

It was at Frankfurt, where he was studying architecture that he developed some intimacy with the Director of a Model School, The Director discovered that true field for Froebel was education. He was advised to give up architecture and join the Model School Froebel found his long-missed life element" and was "inexpressibly happy" with the job of a teacher. He worked there for two years. But he felt he should have more training in the teaching profession. Therefore, he undertook to coach three boys of one family. Feeling dissatisfied with his own work he took his wards to Pestalozzi's school at Yverdun, where he remained for four years. But his desire for knowledge of Natural science carried him in 1811 to Gottimgen University, whence he went to Berlin. Two years later his University studies were interrupted as he joined the Army. Military experience showed him the value of discipline and united action. He realised that the individual belongs not to himself but to the whole body, and how the whole body supports the individual. In 1814 he returned from Military and became a curator of the Museum in Berlin. But the idea of becoming an educator never left him. In 1816 he opened a small school. After passing through many vicissitudes, it became a successful institution in 10 years. It was here in 1826 that Froebel published his great work "The Education of Man".

In 1830 he opened a school in Switzerland, Although the school never flourished, the Swiss Government took advantage of his presence and sent their teachers to him for instruction Soon he moved to Burgdorf to run an orphanage and to superintend the training of teachers for short time course of three months. In his conferences with the teachers he learnt that the schools suffered as they did not get good raw material — the educand. This he believed, was due to no education in the pre-school age.

He had to leave Burgdorf on account of the ill-health of his wife and founded his first Kindergarten in 1839 m the village of Blankenber. His principles of Kindergarten made their headway but his school failed for lack of finances. He brought out "Pedagogics of Kindergarten'. "Education by Development" and "Mother Play and Nursery Songs." The remaining years of his life he continued training teachers and propagating Kindergarten principles. He died on the 21st June 1852.

His Philosophy

His was a philosophy of absolute idealism. In this he assigned a place to education and the development of the individual. The two great ideas that he preached were "unity in diversity" and "his theory of development".

All through his life he went on seeking hidden connections and an underlying unity in all things. He felt that there is an inner connection of the whole cosmical development of the universe. He saw no division in the realm of nature and realm of spirit. He saw no division between the individual and the society.

He viewed the whole universe as a unity from the Absolute or God. He remarked, "In all things there lives and reigns an eternal law. This all controlling law is necessarily based on all pervading, energetic living, self-conscious and hence eternal unity. This unity is God. All things have come from the Divine Unity (God) and have their origin in the Divine Unity. All things, live and have their beings in and through the Divine Unity. The divine affluence that lives in each thing is the essence of each thing." Within this all-inclusive Unity, Froebel included every existing thing *viz.*, man, animal, plant, inanimate object, or human society. Each one of these is an individuality and also a unity. All these individual unities are bound into one great cosmic unity, which may be called God or a spiritual being. He said that "in everything there works and stirs *one* life, because to all, One God has given life."

Both Pestaiozzi and Froebel loved science. Instead of finding science antagonistic to religion, they looked upon it as the expression of the mind of God. God is true and infallible. With this belief Froebel sought to trace everything back to God. He said, "every creature, every object is matter informed by spirit . . . God is the pre-supposition, the condition of their existence. Without God they would not exist. God is the one ground of all things. God is the all comprehending, the all sustaining. God is the essential nature, the meaning of the world."

From this followed his principle that there is a unity of man, nature and God. "Nature and man" seemed to him "mutually explaining each other through all their numberless various stages of development". "Man," as he saw, "received from knowledge of natural objects, even because of their immense deep seated diversity, a foundation for and guidance towards knowledge of himself and life and a preparation for the manifestation of that knowledge. Therefore, Froebel prescribed that man should become conscious of the Absolute unity of universe. He should also know the diversity of things and appearances which are perpetually unfolding themselves within that unity. The varied phenomena in man's life, work, thought and position, he believed, could be summed up in the unity of man's existence. Therefore, the purpose of education, according to him was to expand the life of the individual until it should comprehend this existence through participation in this all pervading spiritual activity.

Like Rousseau and Pestalozzi he also wanted to take shelter in the nature, but his objectives were different. While they believed nature as a great teacher, Froebel wanted that man should become intimate with it not so much with reference to the details and the outer forms of her phenomena as with reference to the spirit of God that lives in her and rules over her. Psychologically he viewed man as a plant developing as a unity according to a law of nature unfolding within him. His theory of development is very dear and consistent. Froebel said that there is an Absolute goal towards which all things are growing. This Absolute is present but only implicitly in every existing thing. Development or growth of anything consists in making this absolute explicit by a gradual unfolding process. The Absolute goal, he said, is realised through the presentation of symbols which represent the various aspects of the Absolute. Without such symbols the conception of the Absolute is not possible. These symbols, he called 'gifts', a reference to which would be made later.

His doctrine of development was that everything develops according to a universal or creative force. May be animal, vegetable or mineral they have a drive to develop along those lines fitted to their characteristics. By development he did not mean, "an increase in bulk or quantity (though it may include this), but an increase in complexity or structure, an improvement in power, skill and variety in the performance of natural functions." To him a thing appeared fully developed, "when its internal organisation is perfect in every detail, and when it can perform all its natural actions or functions perfectly," Applying this theory of development to mind, he said, that mind is developed when it has the power and skill and variety in dealing with knowledge and putting knowledge to all its natural uses.

The development, he was convinced, can be produced by the exercise of function or the use of faculty. Neglect or disuse of any part leads to atrophy and sometimes even the disappearance, of that part. So the faculty must be put to greater use. For this it is essential that the individual should have proper original outfit and then he should get opportunity for exercise. For example, if we wish to develop the hand, we must exercise the hand. Similarly for the development of mind, the mind should be exercised and so on with the development of the body. And again every exercise will not produce development. Only that exercise will produce development which is in harmony with the nature of the thing. To produce true and effective development the exercise must arise from, and be sustained by, the thing's own activity. For example 'mind' has three activities, knowing, feeling and willing. Mental development should be in harmony with all these. The more the activity is that of the whole mind, the more it will be mind's own activity — self-produced, self-maintained and self-directed. Each individual, therefore, must "develop from within, self-active and free, in accordance with the eternal law."

Froebel believed that life is an evolutionary process and opportunity is offered to man to reach higher and higher stages of goodness and perfection through this never ending evolutionary process, Education is the active means in that process. But he held that, "while in every human being there lives humanity as a whole, in each one it is realised and expressed m wholly particular peculiar, personal and unique manner." He maintained that in every person there is at birth a co-ordinated unified plan of his mature character. If it is not marred or unnecessarily interfered with, it would develop naturally of itself. He became a little inconsistent while on the one hand he suggested that natural development must be guided and even shaped, and on the other hand he maintained that "nature is right' and stands for a full and free expression of the instincts and impulses. But he insisted that instruction should not be prescriptive, categorial and interfering. For the full development, Froebel said, it is essential that it should not be brought by imitation or copying but by spontaneous self-activity. He wanted a unified development of the intellectual, physical and moral aspects of man's nature. These he never considered separate. He considered mind, body and soul as one.

His Concept of Education

From his general philosophy followed his concept of education. The school, he said, should not "communicate a variety and multiplicity of facts" bet should teach that there is an everlasting unity in all things. Froebel looked upon the child as an agency for the realisation of God's will in human nature. The spirit of the child, he said, is linked with the spiritual unity of the Absolute through education. Education, he said, is a development by which the individual realises that he is one unit of the all-encompassing, unity. It is "a development by which his life broadens until it has related itself to nature, until it enters sympathetically into all activities of society; until it participates in the achievements of the race and aspirations of humanity." Education, he advocated, is but me realisation of the evolutionary process in its highest stage, which the individual should attain. This process is developed by God. Who develops the most trivial and imperfect things in continuously ascending attain. This development takes place "in accordance with eternal, self-grounded and self-developing laws". Thus he believed that development proceeds through self.

Remarking about the function of education he said, that it, "should lead and guide man to clearness, concerning himself and in himself, to peace with nature, and to unity with God. It should life him to a knowledge of himself and mankind, to a knowledge of god and of nature, and to the pure and holy life." Education must unfold child's innate powers so that he may have a spiritual union with God. He must be treated in such a manner that thus spiritual nature may be awakened. Child, therefore, must be given freedom to develop his energies, his natural curiosity, and his spontaneous activity.

For him education was not a preparation for future life, but the life around him. The school in his opinion is a place where the child learns important things of life, the essentials of truth, justice, free personality, responsibility, initiative and causal relationship. All these the child can learn not by studying about them but by living them and practising them. The school should enable a child to discover his own individuality, work out his own personality and develop his power of initiative and of execution. These the child can achieve through co-operation with others. All children should share interest, responsibility and rewards. Mutual help is the motto of the ideal school of Froebel.

In achieving all these ideals, Froebel assigned a great task to the educator. He has to control the growth of the child into a man, just as the gardener controls the growth of a plant to its full flowering and fruition. The aim of the teacher should be that the child should develop according to his original and logical course of development. Education has failed, if it has neglected or prevented the development of certain sides of the child's nature or if it has caused "the distortion of originally good human powers and tendencies by arbitrary and wilful interference". If the child's nature has somehow been marred, it should be redirected into the original course of development. If the child displays activities contrary to the true principle of growth, they must be recognised and corrected in order to keep the development progressing along the right lines. Thus, according to Froebel, education should be a controlled development.

He saw the problems of education against a sociological background as he remarked, "no community can progress while the individual remains behind; the individual cannot progress while the community remains behind' School has a social significance, as the individuality emerges through the experience of group relationships and activities. Like Pestalozzi he recognized the importance of family education and the link between the home and the school.

The school, he said, was a miniature society. It should be a unified organism in which the units of developing individuality should perfect themselves through participation in the life of the world. The school must produce citizens, who should be ready to put their special abilities to the best service of the community.

Instruction, he commended, should lead from child's spontaneous activities and native interests to some tangible expression of the knowledge. "The education seeks neither to eliminate nature, nor to leave it severely alone." It helps nature and guides it to attain higher ends.

Like Rousseau, Froebel recognises, in education, the stages of development and desires that each one of the stages — infancy, childhood, boyhood and youth — should be fully exploited to prepare the pupil for the succeeding stage. While in infancy he emphasises the sensory development, in childhood his emphasis is on play. While childhood is characterised by making the internal external, in boyhood the process is reversed. Education in boyhood has to be determined by environment and not by endowment as in childhood. Feeling now gives way to thought and play to instruction. It is now to be curriculum-centred and not child-centred. Characteristic activity of childhood was play but that of boyhood should be work. The child takes interest in the process, the boy takes interest in the product. The range of pupil's environment in boyhood widens. This provides him with new pattern of activities in the shape of vocational occupations to be imitated. Of course this work is not those of adults. Learning of some vocation should still be dominated by the spirit of play and not work. The only difference is that in childhood the pupil imitated domestic activities, now he imitates neighbourhood occupations. His activities, now, are projects — practical problems demanding co-operative effort and giving intellectual and moral training.

All-round development being his aim of education, he wanted that the curriculum at the boyhood stage should consist of four main divisions (a) religion, which he says should be the basis of all education. No other knowledge is possible without it. (b) Natural Science: Nature, he has often repeated, is the manifestation of God. Its study will mean the contemplation of outer facts, while religion requires inner contemplation. Therefore both are necessary to have a complete man. Insight into nature reveals the laws that rule in human life. This creates a sense of the reign of law. 'From every object of nature and life there is a way to God". In this study of natural science he also emphasises the importance of mathematics. In his opinion this subject is a connecting link between the mind of man and the natural world. Mind and mathematics, he says, are inseparable as the soul and religion, (c) Languages: these help in establishing the inner living connection among the diversities of things and thus complete the work of education. (d) Expressional work: Froebel believed that there is need for the expression of the soul in outward form. This expression may take the form of singing, drawing, painting and modelling.

His Theory and Practice of Kindergarten

In this conversation with the teachers under training at Burgdorf he learnt that the pre-school age of the children was entirely neglected. His conception of harmonious development led him to attach great importance to early years and his 'The Education of the Man' chiefly deals with the education of children. It became obvious to him that all school education was yet without a proper initial foundation and he realised that until the education of nursery years was reformed nothing solid and worthy could be achieved. It was at Burgdorf that he began to think over the training of children and prepared for them a graduated course of exercises, modelled on the games in which the children were interested.

In 1839, as mentioned earlier, he established his first Kindergarten (a garden in which children are the un-folding plants) in Blankenberg for children between the ages of 3 and 7. He put into use the material he had invented in Burgdorf, added new devices and developed his system. The main features of this were "The play songs" for the mother and child and the series of 'gifts' and 'occupations'. He remained at Blankenberg for seven years and went on expanding his material.

Chief Characteristics of Kindergarten : The Chief characteristics of Froebel's method are, (*a*) self activity; (*b*) creativeness, (*c*) social participation.

By self-activity Froebel meant that the child should not indulge in an activity which is suggested by parents or teacher; but the child should carry out his own impulses and decisions. Education, he believed, is a process of individual growth. This growth is directed by inner forces in the child. This growth of the child differs from that of a plant, as the child has perception and reason. He can be made conscious of the working of God within him. Froebel said that the divine spirit reveals itself in the activities of the child if these activities are spontaneous. By divine law, this free self activity directs growth along the path of racial development. It is this self-activity which merges the child's individuality with the spirit of humanity. Only the teacher should provide appropriate experiences. But the teacher while directing the process must follow nature, never thwart it, for he is but nature's assistant. Education, said Froebel, should not be prescriptive, categorical, interfering, but should provide for "free self-activity and self-determination on the part of man, he being created for freedom in the image of God".

Self-activity helped the instruction to go on steadily, continuously, gradually and inwardly, without any tricks of education like, 'from the simple to the complex' and 'from the concrete to the abstract'. Self-activity in his opinion, is a process by which the individual realises his own nature and builds up his own world and then unites and hormonises the two. The life of the individual is the process by which, (1) he knows nature, or the objective world, (2) comes to know his own nature, and

(3) becomes a part of the life of both nature and humanity. In all this the individual is free and determines his own activities.

Self-activity, therefore, arises out of one's own interests and is sustained by one's own power. It alone can produce the evolution of mind and can secure the aim of education. Since self-activity arises out of inner urges, it can be called free. Since these free activities take place according to the laws of nature, it is possible to formulate them in such a way that they become guide to educational work. It is, therefore, essential that all processes of instruction must originate with the interests of the child. The child must be stimulated to achieve certain ends through spontaneous activities if they are properly directed and influenced by the teacher. Fuller harmony between the inner and the outer, between the thought and the external world cannot be created if the child is not aided by the teacher. Self-activity manifests in the child desire to enter into the life around it, the desire to help, to find out, to discover, and to participate in common activities. The child wants to know the identity or connection between itself and the activities of others. Froebel said there is no hiatus between knowledge and action, no conflict between theory and practice and no discrepancy between profession and deeds.

With self-activity is connected Froebel's principle of 'creativeness'. Through creativeness new forms and combinations are made and expression is given to new images and ideas. He said "plastic-material-representation in life and through doing, united with thought and speech, is by far more developing and cultivating than the merely verbal representation of ideas". Man is, he said, by nature an active and dynamic being. He is not a receptive and passive observer of events. He must create.

Froebel recognised the unitary character of human nature and its growth through the activity of all of his parts. Head, soul and hand are inseparable. They are inter-dependent parts of man and must be developed together. Mind and soul express themselves and grow through bodily activity and expression. He condemned intellectualism and verbalism and advocated that thinking must express itself in doing, otherwise education would remain unproductive.

Rousseau had advocated isolated and un-social education for 'Emile' but Froebel laid great emphasis on the social aspect of education. He held that increasing self-realisation or individualisation through self-activity comes through a process of socialisation. Social instinct being a primary instinct of man, the individual can be truly educated only in the company of the other human beings. Man's life is bound up with participation in institutional life. The home, the school, the church, the vocation, the state — all are the medium for individual activity and a means of social control. The school, Froebel said, is an association for the child wherein he discovers in a simplified and idealised form the relations of society. It is a means of social progress and individual development. Similarly in the society a child receives the development and also prepares for the future life. Through imitation of co-operative activities in play he obtains not only physical but intellectual and moral training. His growth, therefore, should be in harmony with the unity and purposes of humanity to which he belongs.

Froebel's Kindergarten is a miniature state for children. There, the young citizens learn to move freely, but with a consideration for each other. It is a school without books. There are no set intellectual tasks. It is permeated with play, freedom and joy. Self-activity, creativeness and social co-operation find complete application and concrete expression. The training in a Kindergarten consists of three co-ordinate forms of expression (1) song (2) movement (3) construction. Out of these, there automatically grows the use of language by the child. All these are separate but they often co-operate with one another and interpret one another. The whole process becomes one organic whole. For example, when the story is told or read it is first expressed in song, then it is dramatised in movement and gesture and finally it is illustrated by constructive work from blocks, paper clay or other material. In this way ideas are given, "thought stimulated, the imagination vivified, the hands and eyes trained, the muscles co-ordinated and the moral nature strengthened." In the Kindergarten all efforts are put into concrete, objective form. The higher motives and sentiments are aroused.

All the songs are about common objects of life. They are intended to exercise the infant's senses, limbs and muscles. Every song must relate a nursery game and must correspond to a special, physical, mental and moral need of the child. The selection, and order of the songs is determined according to the development of the child. Each song of Froebel contained three parts (*a*) a motto for the guidance of the mother (*b*) a verse with accompanying music, to sing to the child (*c*) a picture illustrating the verse.

The fundamental thought of the Kindergarten is to help the child to express himself and thus produce development. For this, start has to be made with his innate interest and tendency. The work of the school is based upon self-activity and ends in the expression or use of the ideas or knowledge acquired during the course of the activity. The main object is not the acquisition of knowledge but growth or development. Knowledge is only a means to an end. It is subordinate and by-product, although very essential for the growth. Acquisitive and assimilative processes are the preliminary stages to constructive process.

The teacher's part in Kindergarten is to organise and guide the free and continuous development of the pupil through play. His study of children showed him that a child is restless both of body and mind. Children, he said, are anxious to move their limbs and their mind. They are curious to know. It was, why he devised gifts and occupations. They are introduced gradually and in order. As the child becomes familiar with the characteristics of one gift or one activity, he is led on to the next, which grows out of the previous one, introducing new impression and repeating old ones.

Gifts and occupations were meant to stimulate activity. The gifts combine and re-arrange certain definite material without changing the form, while the 'occupation' re-shape, modify, and transform their material.

The first gift is a box of six woollen balls of different colours. They are to be rolled about in play and thus develop the child's ideas about colour, material, form, motion, direction and muscular sensibility. Froebel would give the ball to the child at the age of three months. This would lead the child immediately to play. The ball symbolises the unity of the Universe and the child's own nature. It elicits in him his own inner idea of that unity and his participation in it. The game of the ball stimulates and trains the senses and muscles and his power of attention. It also infuses in the child confidence in his own ability. The moving ball, sometimes in his grasp and sometimes out of it would teach him the meaning of such things as space, time, the past, present and future. The mother or the teacher sings in imitation and description of the motion of the ball. The child learns the meaning of the words 'up', 'down' , 'out', 'around', etc. As the child grows older, the motion of the ball becomes a symbol of life.

The 2nd gift is a Sphere, Cube, and Cylinder or hard wood. They help him in comparing the stability of the cube with the movability of the sphere. The child also learns that the two are harmonised in the cylinder. The handling of a ball or sphere is supposed to give the child the sense of the perfect unity of all things. Sitting in a circle also makes the child feel his identification as an individual with a social group. Thus he is led to realise the unity of all mankind in the Absolute.

A large wooden cube divided into 8 equal cubes is the third gift. It helps in teaching the child the relation of the parts to the whole and to one another and also makes possible many original constructions.

The other three gifts divide the cube in various ways in order to produce solid bodies of different types and sizes and thus they excite an interest in number, relation and form. From these the children are encouraged to construct geometrical figures and artistic designs. There are still other gifts for later stages. They are square and triangular tablets, sticks and rings.

Froebel's 'occupations,' are as important as are 'gifts'. They comprise a long list of construction with paper, sand, clay, wood and other materials. There are many others like mat and paper weaving, stick shaping, sewing, bead-threading, paper-pricking and drawing. The gifts and occupations all lead to the closer identification of the child with the divine spirit and social unity.

Importance of play: After many forms of free self-activity, the play of the childhood is of paramount importance. It is a nature's way of directing the growth of the child according to social pattern. This being a prime native tendency of the child, it can be best utilised for inculcating in the child the habits of action, fleeing and thought. Through play the educator can give to the child the interpretation of life. The child can be taught social relations, independence and mutual helpfulness. Play enables children to achieve confidence and balance in an orderly world. Initiative and motivation are developed in him. Thus is developed an individual constituting a unit in the social whole.

The child observes the world and imitates it in play. Froebel says that play is "self-active representation of the inner necessity and impulse. Play is the purest, most spiritual activity of man ......

it gives, therefore, joy, freedom, contentment, inner and outer rest, peace with the world. It holds the source of all that is good."

Froebel erased the distinction between play and work. These two are one. Education, he said, should not be soft, but it must be playful.

Value of hand work : In Frobel's Kindergarten all constructive work makes an idea or a process of instruction real. He said that constructive work should be the beginning and the end of the educational process. Rousseau recognised industrial training on social and economic grounds. Pestalozzi introduced manual activities for developing sense perception. Froebel emphasised the manual and industrial training because it gave expression to an idea or purpose. All constructive work, he believed, manifests outwardly what the child feels inwardly. Such manifestation of ideas are the basis of the higher power of expressing the intellectual, moral and spiritual life in action.

Nature Study : Similarly he commends the introduction of nature study in the school curriculum. By prescribing the study he was the least concerned with the facts about nature. He desired that the child should "have moral improvement, religious uplift and spiritual insight" by coming into contact with nature. Nature study afforded the child opportunity for varied activity. It suggests material for reading, writing, language work; constructive work, and number work. He does not want nature to be analysed and dissected. He wants to study nature "as life — the plant as development, the animal as acting — the organ as functioning."

To sum up it can be said that the aim of Kindergarten was individual development. The method was motor expression and self-activity. The means were social co-operation.

His Contribution

Froebel was a person who never ceased "to systematise, symbolise, idealise, realise and recognise identities and analogies" among all facts and phenomena of the universe. He made life "more simple and clear and more recognisable". He had a living perception of universal and ideal truth. He had un-bounded enthusiasm for the education and happiness of human race. Such an educator could not fail to attract and elevate the posterity. "All the best tendencies of modern thought in education. . . culminate in what was said and done by Froebel. He has shown the right road for further advance". Can there be any better tribute paid to Froebel than this?

Although Froebel himself said that centuries would pass before his views "of the human creature as manifested in the child, and of the educational treatment it required "would be universally received," yet it can be seen that Froebelian Kindergarten soon caught the eye of the educational world and now the cult of the Kindergarten has come to stay. Since his death Kindergarten school has sprung up rapidly in all the progressive countries of the world. Many tendencies in the curricula and methods of the school today can be traced back to him. He has given his theory and practice for a period of life of the child, hitherto very largely neglected. Being a very close student of children, his study of them was such as had never been done before. To him the child was inherently good and he studied the individual differences of the children in order to be guided in their educative process. Recognising the importance of the native capacities of children he advocated a sympathetic regard for these, both by parents and teachers. It was he, who created a new respect for the individuality of the child. He realised the value of discovering and developing the individuality by means of initiative, execution and co-operation in educational process. Since then these have become the bywords in educational theory and practice. He has inspired the various arts and crafts like clay-modelling etc., in the modern education. His emphasis upon activity and social participation and a school without books and set tasks, was a unique contribution to educational practice. He impressed upon the world that rigid discipline and the traditional formality of the school atmosphere must be given up to develop the dynamic and active qualities of child's nature.

His emphasis upon the manipulation of objects and freedom to explore and express oneself produced a greater attention to activity and sense realism in place of the constant and regimented reading of books. The child, he said, is "replete with all the active tendencies of human nature". The notion of group activity as a natural means of expression led to the realisation of the importance of good social relationship as a desirable result of school and community life.

With Froebel the full social significance of education is fuzzy grasped. He wanted the education to fit the individual for full life within the group and aimed to open up to pupils the whole wide range of human knowledge and experience. It is the working out this conception that forms the chief concern of education today.

No phase of school, work has so closely 'approximated the idea of society in microcosm' as has the Kindergarten.

His view that education is a growth and a growth from within of the native powers of child held a great influence on the later thought of teaching theory and practice. His doctrine that knowledge is not the end of education but the means towards the end, minimised the value of verbalism. His recognition of the educational value of play, self-activity, creative work, social participation, and learning by doing are psychologically, socially and practically sound. They have been embodied in educational practices from the infant schools to Universities.

He was a great exponent of the fundamental use of play and education. But he believed in guided and progressive activities. It was on account of purposeful activity that he identified play and work as one. Froebel was the first to take the formative and creative instincts of children into account for education. His doctrine of play has had the greatest influence upon educational practice. It formed the centre of new education. Its spirit runs into project method and in the whole range of experimental and creative activities of the modern progressive schools.

Kindergarten has been declared to be, "by far the most original, attractive and philosophical form of infant development, the world has yet seen" and it has spread in all progressive lands. Froebel completed the system of Rousseau by providing the richer and more stimulating environment which was denied to 'Emile.'

Froebel adopted Pestalozzi's objective methods of teaching geography, natural history, arithmetic, drawing, writing, reading and constructive geometry. Like Rousseau he believed, that nature is infallible and advocated the physical training and excursion as means of study.

In conclusion it may be seen that it was Froebel who said that education is a natural process, that child is an organic whole itself and is an organic part of the society and that the whole universe is an organism of which all lesser organisms are members. His faith in man's relationship with nature, his advanced scientific thought, his belief that universe has emerged by a process of evolution with which the education should be in harmony were his greatest contributions. He was the first educational evolutionist. Education to him was the process by which the race and the individual evolve to higher and higher levels.

4

Dr. Maria Montessori

(1870—1952)

Further experiments in using the self-activity and creative energies of children to the fullest possible extent were undertaken in the twentieth century by an Italian lady, Madame Montessori by name.

Dr. Montessori, who served the cause of education throughout the first half of the twentieth century was born in 1870. When she was young she was very emotional but had a powerful intellect. At first she wanted to become an actress and actually joined a dramatic school. Soon, however, she realised that her mission of life was different and she decided to take up medicine. In those days it was difficult for a woman to join a medical college. She found her way to the college in an interesting manner. When she applied for admission she signed herself 'M. Montessori.' Since the authorities could never think that a woman would apply, they admitted her thinking her to be man. She was thus the first Italian woman to get the degree of Doctor of Medicine.

From 1900 to 1907 she remained a professor of Anthropology in the University of Rome. Here she took a special interest in the mentally deficient children and also studied the psychology of childhood. This study enabled her to form an opinion that mental deficiency resulted, from the dullness of senses. A proper sense training, therefore, she said, would enable the deficient children to acquire some knowledge.

Seeing the plight of children of working women, she opened a children's home. In it she collected the children of the poor people, kept them amused by playing with them and also imparted them sense training. She made certain things with her own hands in order to find some method of teaching them, because they were not intelligent enough to learn in the old way with books. She discovered that the means of playing began to reveal something thrilling. She found in this new way the children learnt eagerly, enthusiastically and intelligently. She says, "nothing in fact is so fascinating as to attend the mental awakening of these children who are enslaved by their own inferiority, and to witness this kind of liberation of the soul from extinction through spiritual poverty, to see them arise, reviving and opening up towards interest that gave life to their intelligence, to witness the happiness that comes to them through every activity in which the hand becomes capable of achieving something. It is really man arising from death to the joy of living". Thus her work began. It was after that, that she produced several books on educational reform *viz.* 'The Discovery of the Child', 'Education for a New World', 'To Educate the Human Potential', 'The Secret of Childhood', 'The Absorbent Mind', 'What you should know about your Child', 'Child Training'; 'The Montessori Method', 'The Child Peace and Education', and 'Reconstruction in Education'.

In 1922 she was appointed Inspectress of Infant Schools by her Government. She also began to impart training to teachers not in her own country but in many countries of Europe, including England. The Durham University conferred on her the honorary Degree of Doctor of Letters.

When Mussolini became the dictator of Italy, he did not agree with her method of education to develop the individuality of the child. He wanted her to educate the young for war. She left Italy, went to Spain and started her work there. But she had to leave the country when that country turned Fascist. Thence, she proceeded to Holland, where she founded a school. In 1939 she came to India and remained here up to 1951, conducting several training courses for teachers of young children. It was on May 6, 1952, that she breathed her last in Holland.

The 'Forgotten Citizens'

Montessori called the children as 'forgotten citizens' and felt that they deserved much more careful consideration than was or is being generally given to them. The child should be taken up, she said, when he has not yet acquired the muscular co-ordination, when his sensory organs are not yet developed, when his emotional life is unstable and has not yet developed his will power. She held that a "Consciously controlled and systematically directed" education in childhood would yield astonishing results. She said that each child should be treated as an individual and be allowed to progress at his own rate. All children cannot be expected to learn the same things at the same time and at the same speed. She believed that there is a psychological moment for doing everything. In the educative process this moment comes when the child feels the inner urge for doing a thing. "It is necessary", she said, "to offer those exercises which correspond to the need of development felt by organism. If the child's age has carried him past a certain need, it is never possible to obtain, in its fullness, a development which missed its proper moment." Therefore, she advised the Directress of the Montessori School to keep a constant eye on the psychological needs of individual children.

The child, she realised, is not the child. He is the whole man — the complete past, present and future in a young body. Within that young body are the seeds of qualities of weakness of capacities and of intelligence. She understood the mischievious child and discovered what is mischief. She understood the process of the child's growth. She says, "Education cannot exist other than in a dynamic state, in a continuous transformation of the individual who is to be raised to a higher level. This process must develop in accordance with the inner dictates of life. It is the creative force which must develop and we (teachers and parents) must not make ourselves substitutes, in an arbitrary manner, for the divine work which is accomplished in every living being. Indeed, we cannot be more than co-operators in educational work with creation. We cannot force the child to follow our promptings, but we must provide the means best adapted to help the child in his voluntary work." She, therefore, wants the careful organisation of the child's environment, the regulation of his liberty, and. the provision of the special material for his use, designed to give him practice and activities which might otherwise be encountered in the environment only accidentally or casually.

Her Principles of Education

By education, she understood "the active help given to the normal expansion of the life of the child." Child, she said, should be able to adjust himself to his immediate environment. She was an environmentalist and believed that a well constituted environment will develop within the child that 'active' life, which will give him pleasure and will also reveal to him a spiritual life. Freedom and auto-education should be the mottos of that environment. She wanted the development of the child from within and not from without. Latent powers of the child, she advocated, must be unfolded. This was responsible for her faith in individual instruction rather than in class teaching. She would have a class only as a unit of organisation, and not as a unit of teaching. "The child," She said, "is a body which grows and a soul which develops". Such a mysterious thing, therefore, should neither be marred nor stifled. Educational activities should be so planned that a child's individuality must be unfolded to the full. The child, she held, is gifted at birth to become something. The teacher, therefore, should guide in such a way that the child's hidden powers are realised by him. This would enable the child to acquire new knowledge and learn new skills. In this process the educator should play the part of a guide and organiser. He or she should remain in the background, not as a passive observer but as an active wire-puller. The educator should have "anxious scientific curiosity" about the child.

For the education of the child she devised a "Didactic apparatus" or developmental material. Originally intended for mental defectives, the Didactive apparatus was applied by Montessori to the normal children. This is an apparatus which can be used by the children themselves without help from the teacher. After trying the "apparatus" with normal children she formulated four principles.

1. Education must always be an individual business. Montessori believed that every human being has his own peculiar native powers and develops them in his own peculiar way when put on spontaneous activities. She rang a death-knell to collective or class teaching and wanted the child to be guided individually. Intimate touch, she said, with the mental and physical development of the child, would very much facilitate the work of the teacher in individual guidance.

While she emphasised individual and independent action, she was not unmindful of the social needs and of the task of improving society. She says, "The discipline to which the child habituates himself here (school) is, in its character, not limited to the school environment but extends to society."

2. Individual development is best directed by means of a graded series of educational apparatus. This she provided in abundance, as we shall see later.

3. All education should be self education. Through self education and at his own rate child learns best: Constant interference of the teacher is strictly prohibited by Montessori. She has tried to eliminate the teacher's interference as much as she could. Her Didactic apparatus controls every error and the child is always in a Position to correct himself. She said that if a child fails to do a thing or fails to appreciate the truth of a principle, it is not for the teacher to repeat the lesson. She should think that the thing has been presented prematurely and should await the time, when the child manifests the inner urge for learning that thing. In a Montessorian school a child may be seen working for several days on a self-imposed task. In her school there is no place for rewards and no unnecessary competition. Sense of achievement is the only reward. Self-development is the greatest pleasure.

4. For the self-education the children should have the necessary freedom and impersonal directress instead of ordinary teacher. Freedom, she said, is the fundamental right of every human being. Spontaneous development can take place only if there is no restraint. The school, therefore, must permit, "the free and natural manifestations of the child," if a scientific study of the child has to be made. Her freedom is subject to absolute obedience to the laws of development of child's nature. There is freedom of pupils in their spontaneous expression. It was, why she advocated free discipline.

Practices in the House of Childhood

Froebel called the asylum of children the Kindergarten. Montessori called it "House of Childhood". Atmosphere and environment are the two great factors in the House. It should provide all the necessaries of living, a garden to play and a number of rooms for lunch, work, games, amusement, rest, etc.

The programme of activities in the House comprises of three types (1) daily life exercises; (2) sense training exercises; (3) Didactic exercises.

Daily Life Exercises : Taking care of themselves is the first phase. It is based upon freedom of doing one's own job. The children are taught to act independently. For example, they are required to look to their personal cleanliness and hygiene. They learn how to use the wash basin, how to clean their nails, brush their teeth and polish their shoes. They are required to dust their own rooms, arrange their own furniture, set and serve their own tables and wash their own clothes. Dressing and undressing is taught to them by means of an apparatus. This consists of a "wooden frame, mounted with two pieces of cloth or leather, which are fastened by means of buttons and button-holes, hooks and eyes, eye-lets, and lacings or automatic fasteners". Practice on this apparatus teaches the child to dress and undress himself independently. Similarly the furniture — chairs, tables, cup-boards — is of a special size and construction and it can very conveniently be handled by children themselves. Moving it in and out teaches them motor adjustment. Everything that is used by children is, as suits their handling. In this way they manage their own affairs of life in their own environment, specially designed for them. Even gardening is done by small children.

In order to develop the co-ordinated movements of the child, Montessori devised certain gymnastic exercises, suiting to their age. For example, she has a spiral stair made of wood. On one side of the stair there is balustrade and the other side is open. Children keep their hand on the balustrade and climb up and down the stairs. This they have to do in a balanced and self-controlled manner. The steps on the stair are convenient to the children and are unlike those which we have usually in our homes meant for adults. Such an exercise produces in them gracefulness of carriage.

Sense Training : Like Rousseau, Pestalozzi and Froebel, she also subscribed to the view that the senses are the gateways of knowledge. Therefore their appropriate training is essential to acquire knowledge. To her, sensory discrimination is more important than reasoning and thinking. Self-education is possible only through the development of senses. Her system of education, therefore, began with the training of senses. For this, she employs various material : Through the regular graded use of this material children gain skills of manipulation and judgement through the senses. Physical and intellectual development is also associated through this training. The sense of touch, for example, may be developed by asking the child to put his hand in the water of different degrees of warmth. A highly polished surface and sand paper surface may also be used for the same purpose. For perception of size, series of wooden cylinders are used. They vary in height and in diameter or in both dimensions at once. Similarly blocks of varying sizes and rods of regularly graded lengths may be used. Auditory acuity is developed by boxes, which may be full of pebbles or any other material producing sound. Wooden tablets of different weights, but having the same size may be used for developing the sense of weight. There is provided a graded series of coloured wools for developing the colour sense. The children are required to sort and grade 64 cards of various colours of wool.

Montessori attached the greatest importance to the development of sense of perception of 'form'. For this various types of material are used. Children may be required to sort out of a heap of bricks and cubes. They recognise the form by grasping them. Sometimes coins are also used for the same purpose. The children become so expert in perceiving the form that they can distinguish even smallest things such as corn, wheat and rice. Real training in perception of form is given through geometrical insets made of metal or wood. The children must be able to place metal or wooden shapes in spaces made to receive them or they should be able to superimpose such shapes on outlines of similar form. Geometric insets of various designs are mixed up. Children sort them and fit them into the frames made to receive them. The three-fold process of visual, tactual, and muscular sense helps the perception of the form and fixes it in the memory. The next exercise pertains to wooden insets being superimposed on figures cut out of cardboard. Finally, the child superimposes the wooden pieces on figures represented by lines. This is how the child proceeds from "the concrete to the abstract", "from solid objects to plain figures", represented by lines and perceived by vision alone. In this way he also gets the idea about circle, ellipse, triangle and rectangle etc. By this method, however, the intention is not to teach them geometry so much as to give them perception of form.

Didactic exercises : After sense training children are taught writing, reading and arithmetic (counting). On account of preparatory sense training, self education in these three fundamental skills goes on quite smoothly.

She gave precedence to writing over teaching of reading, because she felt that muscles are developed in infancy and they make the teaching of writing easy. Reading involves the science of modulation of voice and accentuation of syllables. It is purely an intellectual task and requires high intellectual development. While writing is a task of motor adjustment, the procedure of teaching writing was drawn by Montessori from her experience with a mentally deficient girl whom she taught sewing. She inferred that repeated exercises with hand would give that facility of movement by which the form of letters is reproduced. For writing she uses the same procedure as she followed in developing the perception of form, described above. The fingers of children have already been exercised on geometric insets. Montessori got the shapes of letters cut out in sand-paper, pasted them on cards and then the pupils were required to pass their fingers over them. After acquiring facility in thus tracing the form of letter, the children take pleasure in repeating the movement with fingers in the air with closed eyes. Unlike the traditional method of learning the letters by "visual analysis and retained by visual imagery", they learn by "tactual and motor experiences and graphomotor imagery". When the tracing of letter form is going on, the sounds are given and thus the way is prepared for the teaching of reading.

In order to teach the child the control of pen, the child is required to take up a metal frame into which the inset fits. He draws the metal frame on a sheet of paper with a coloured crayon. In this figure he places the metal inset and with a crayon of a different colour traces the outline of the inset. Thus two figures are produced in different colours upon the paper. With another crayon the pupil fills in these figures. In making the upward and downward strokes the child is taught not to pass outside the contour. By practice the lines tend less and less to go outside the sketches. Thus the child has learnt writing. This perfection in writing is attained by three-fold process: (1) control of pen; (2) eproducing the forms of letters by moving his fingers in the air; and (3) composing words out of the isolated sounds of letters. Montessori said that the average time required between the preparatory exercises and the written work is 30 to 45 days for a child of 4 years. With a child of 5 the period is still less.

Reading is also taught in the same way as writing. Technically it demands the reproduction of the sounds from the symbols and the fusion of these sounds into words. For the correct pronunciation of the word, proper accentuation of the syllable is essential. This comes only with the recognition of the meaning. Montessori said, "Reading is the interpretation of an idea from the written signs. Until the child reads the transmission of ideas from the words, he does not read. In her Didactic material, reading lessons consist of slips of papers or cards upon which words and phrases are written in clear and large script. At first the names of familiar objects are given. The directress gives a card to the child, he utters the sounds and this is fixed in the memory by repeating it faster and faster. When the child is able to pronounce the word he is asked to place the card under the object whose name it bears. Similarly, sentences describing action or expressing commands are written on the slips of paper. The child selects one of these and does the action contained in that. He does not read the sentence because Montessori believed that reading should be silent and not vocal. "Reading aloud", according to her, "implies the exercise of two mechanical forms of language — articulate and graphic — and is a complex task". She, therefore, wanted that reading should be done mentally. According to her the average time required for learning to read is about a fortnight after the child has learnt the process of writing.

In teaching counting she uses a long stair. It is a set of ten rods, the first being one metre in length, the last, one decimetre and the middling rods decreasing in length by decimetres. Each rod is divided into portions of one decimetre each. These portions are alternately painted red and blue. The child is first given practice in arranging the rods in order of length. He is then required to count the red and the blue divisions. By thus manipulating the rods all the four fundamental rules (addition, subtraction, multiplication and division) of arithmetic are taught. The graphic signs for the numbers are cut in sand-paper and the pupils are taught to associate the numbers with their graphic form.

The Place of Teacher

To give training on Montessorian line there is a need for a special type of teacher. The teacher, here, is different from that of an ordinary school and that is why Montessori prefers to call her a directress rather than a teacher. She insists, "the broader the teacher's scientific culture and practice in experimental psychology, the sooner will come for her the marvel of unfolding life, and her interest in it." A full understanding of experimental psychology will enable the teacher to give an ideal lesson. Here the teacher has to observe the psychic development of the child and had to direct him accordingly. She should know when to interfere and when not to interfere with the activity of the child. She has only to observe and intervene when absolutely necessary.

The teacher must allow full freedom to the child and this is what Montessori means by free discipline. It should not be imposed from an external agency. The observance of law or rule should arise from the inner urge of the child. The teacher should play a three-fold role. She should be a doctor, who refrains from scolding or suppressing the patient in order to avoid worst situation. She should be a scientist and wait for the result patiently doing experiment with her material. She should be a religious lady to whom the service of the child should be uppermost.

Her Contribution

The work of Dr. Maria Montessori have had considerable influence in developing the nursery school. Her artistic imagination, sensitiveness, childlikeness and profound sympathy opened a new vista for the child. Her gospel of love and reverence towards the child has been accepted by the world. She brought to the world of education the knowledge that even a child of two is mature within the circumstances of his being or intelligence. Only his is a different approach and he has different ways of learning. It was, why she created a new way of learning — called the Montessori system.

The Montessori system has become so popular that the word "Montessori" has become synonymous with "child". There may be many who do not realise that there was such a person as Dr. Montessori. She devised really a form of learning that Nature made it possible for the child. Only she wanted the teacher, "filled with a mystic ardour", following "all the revelation of the little child's mind". She desired that the teacher, at first, must aspire for her own perfection and then she, "may carry her perfection into the beautiful workroom of a class-room peopled with little children. She brought joy and happiness to every school and every class. If the children in certain schools today go eagerly to classes, to learn mathematics or geography or any other subject with the least fear, it is entirely due to Montessori. All values of Montessori methods have been absorbed by the modern Kindergarten and nursery schools.

Her most valuable contribution to educational progress is the idea of individual, education, guided by carefully planned material which has been graded in accordance with school-room experiment and experience. In the words of Curtis, Montessori was "a Catholic a democrat and a scientist. As a Catholic she could not be pragmatist (or naturalist. As a democrat she upheld individual liberty and sought to foster the full and free development of children. As a scientist she aimed to educate through realities — by providing concrete material and by organising learning situations for pupils".

To her "the child was God. Her school was the temple and deity of the temple was the essence of childhood". If such an attitude is imbibed by the teacher to-day, educational millennium is a certainty.

Limitations of her Methods

She gives little importance to the play activities of children. Similarly the inter-play of the individual and group is not emphasised by her.

A little too much importance was given to the apparatus which she devised. Self-education by this becomes a mechanical thing. Practical life activities are not provided by the manipulation of Didactic apparatus. Exercises with it are so limited that children cannot fully express themselves. Similarly the apparatus also limits the scope of work by the teacher, because it is error-proof. His own imagination does not get full expression in teaching the children.

Montessori has taken good care of the development of the physical personality of the child, but psychological aspects of temperament and character have been ignored.

Her too much emphasis upon the training of sense is not acceptable to the modern psychologists, who believe that besides the training of senses, there is a place for imagination and phantasy, judgement and comparison. It would have been much better if she had designated sense training as "perceptual training".

The materials and methods employed by Montessori are little more than a development of the Kindergarten. For some time there was a good deal of enthusiasm for Montessorian method but later lanalysis of the fundamental ideas revealed that her method was based on the outdated "faculty psychology". The interest, therefore, decreased.

Froebel and Montessori Compared

The attractions of present-day progressive and happy schools are due to the common-sense of Montessori and wisdom of Froebel. Froebel believed in the natural gifts and the endowment of the child, while Montessori was environmentalist. She considered environment as very important for the education of the child.

While Froebel advocated the use of fairy tales, fables and fantasy for stimulating the imagination of the child, Montessori system had no place for them. She wanted the imagination to be developed through realities as "the imagination of modern men is based upon the positive researches of science". But does not deny that in art, music, poetry and also in morality and religion" there is a creative work which lifts man up from earth and transports him to a higher world which every soul may attain within its individual limits". The Kindergartener is a teller of stories as well as a group leader and organiser of short time activities. The Montessorian directress is an observer of individuals who select their own activities and decide for themselves when to change. Montessori school, therefore, requires much more apparatus than Kindergarten.

Froebel's children carry on group activities, Montessori wants the individual child to do his own task in his own way at his own speed. Froebel gave physical training through group work, Montessori through specially designed apparatus. The former advocates the classroom teaching according to time-table. No such restrictions are prescribed by the latter. Unlike Froebel, she does not attach much importance to play, except that which she thinks necessary for motor adjustments or for handling the Didactic apparatus. On the other hand every lesson in Kindergarten is taught in a play-way method, whose chief essentials are song, movement and gesture. In the House of Childhood great prominence is given to daily routine of life like dressing, undressing, laying and dusting of furniture and not much importance is attached to manual activities like gardening, clay modelling, paper cutting etc. which are emphasised in the Kindergarten.

Both of them emphasised the training of sense but they differ in their degree of emphasis.

Kindergarten teacher is supposed to interfere sufficiently in order to guide his pupils, while in Montessori school teacher remains in the background and free discipline is inculcated.

5

John Dewey

(1859—1952)

While Madame Montessori stressed the importance of utilising to the fullest possible the senses, the social aspects of education did not receive her special attention. It was left to Dewey to stress that education is a process of living in a society.

John Dewey, the American Philosopher, Psychologist and practical teacher was born in Vermont in New England in 1859. He was the son of a shopkeeper and was brought up in rural environment. The experience of early years brought to him two convictions:

(1) that traditional methods of schooling were useless, and (2) that human contracts of everyday life provide unlimited, natural dynamic learning situations. He heard the shrewd lively comments and discussions in his father's shop and realised the strength and power of group consciousness in the various activities of small society. These two convictions, as would be seen in this chapter, directed the course of his educational work.

He graduated from the University of Vermont in 1879, studied philosophy for another year, remained teacher for a brief spell and then proceeded to Johns Hopkins University. After two years he got his Ph.D. here and became a lecturer in philosophy at the University of Michigan, where he remained till 1894. In that year he was appointed the head of the Department of Philosophy in the University of Chicago. From 1902 to 1904 he was also the Director of the School of Education. In 1896 he founded his 'laboratory school' in the University. It was the school which brought him world fame. All his theories were tested in this school. His concepts of education were modified and clarified in the light of practical experience of the school situation.

In 1904 he became Professor of Philosophy at the Columbia University. This position he held up to 1930 and then he became Professor Emeritus, until he died in 1952. During his assignment at Columbia University, he undertook educational engagements and commissions abroad. In 1919 he lectured on the philosophy and education at the University of Tokyo and then he spent two years at Peking University. In the thirties he was invited by the Turkish Government to report on the reorganisation of Turkish schools.

His Laboratory School

John Dewey's promotion of educational theory and practice originated in an experimental school opened in the University of Chicago, in 1896. The school was officially called the University Elementary school. Its main purpose was to carry on research and experiment in new ideas and methods of education. Children between the ages of 4 and 14 were admitted. Experienced teachers were appointed. The direction and supervision of the school was under John Dewey. The classes were small. That was the first ideal. Not more than 8 to 10 pupils were given to each teacher. But the curriculum followed was that of a traditional primary school. Dewey's aim was to "create the conditions for the discovery of more natural ways of teaching and learning." Given the equipment and freedom from mass instruction the teachers were required to discover ways and means of breaking down the barriers between school and community life.

Dewey realised that great social and industrial changes had taken place in American life. He, therefore, wished to bring the children in his school into touch with the world around them. To him the ordinary schools had failed to keep pace with the extraordinary changes brought in the society by the Industrial Revolution. Such schools had served the people well as long as most of them were country dwellers. But now that the people had shifted to the towns they required a different type of training. Industries being the most fundamental in the thought, ideals and social organisation of a pupil, these activities, he thought should be prominent in the school. He remarked, "The school cannot be a preparation for social life, except as it reproduces the typical conditions of life." To him the material for providing this industrial activity was mainly shop work, cooking, sewing and weaving, although many subsidiary activities were also undertaken. Such training, he believed, enabled the children to engage in social life in the miniature. "The school," he said, "is not a preparation for life; it is life". The occupations in his school were intended to have liberalising influence. They were not taught as technical subjects. Teachers were required to find ways of including a richer, more varied subject matter in pupil's studies without adding to the burden of rote learning and symbol interpretation. They were required to make the acquirement of basic skills more interesting. The three R's were not neglected. They were also to be developed more effectively as the pupils were made to feel that they were necessary in our studies. Similarly play, observation, hand work and stories representing real life also constituted the important portion of curriculum.

The school was a community, where learning was an active and co-operative process involving investigation, construction and artistic creation. From these arose "plenty of opportunities and occasions" for the use of number, reading, writing and spelling. They were not treated as subjects but rather organic phases of the child's continuous experience. Singing, drawing and dramatisation was encouraged. Children's social relationships were also attended to. Speaking about the general principles of a school Dewey said, "that: (1) the primary object of the school is to train children in co-operative and mutually helpful living, (2) educative activity lies in the instructive and impulsive attitudes and activities of the child, and not in the presentation of subject matter, and (3) the individual tendencies and activities are organised and directed through co-operative living". The activities and occupations of the society were reproduced in the school on the child's plane.

This school was experimental in two senses. (1) It made constant use of experiment and enquiry about the children's methods of learning, (2) It was a laboratory for the transformation of school into a miniature society. Children at the age of 6 began with home activities. In the following years the historical development of industry, invention and group living was followed. Since man depended upon nature and upon society, the pupils were required to study science and history.

The teaching was done by means of problems arising in life situations. For example, the study of cotton was carried through all stages from the seed and growing plant, the matured fibre, spinning and weaving to the use of the finished cloth. Old and new inventions were studied. The presence of clocks and telephones led to the study of communication and social co-operation. "Blind effort, formal drill, recitation and overt discipline were eliminated by guiding the children in self-education through discovery, construction and co-operation". Dewey's aim was to develop thought and test it by action, as he believed that only the tested thought is real knowledge. About this experimental school he himself said, "in intent whatever the failures, in accomplishment the school was community-centred".

His Writings

The educational philosophy practised and developed in the laboratory school was embodied by Dewey in all his works on education. His first educational work came out in 1896 known as "Interest as Related to Will". The very next year saw the publication of "My Pedagogic Creed". "The School and Society" was published in 1899. In all these works he stated his general theory of education. In them was manifest a revolt against the traditional aims of education of the 19th century. He was opposed to the religiously motivated moral aim, disciplinary aim and the informative aim — all of which were considered the aims of education in the 19th century. He said that schools should strive to elevate the aims of civic and social experience, vocational and practical usefulness and the individual development.

The outline of thought contained in these works forms the ground work of Dewey's philosophy of education. In the first half of the 20th century, this was further elaborated and about four dozen books on philosophy, psychology, education, ethics and even politics came out. Most well-known on education are: 'Relation of Theory to Practice in the Education of Teachers' (1904); "*The School and the Child*' (1907); '*Moral Principles in Education*' (1909); '*How we Think*' (1910); '*Schools of Tomorrow*' (1915); '*Democracy and Education*' (1916); '*Education To-day*' (1940).

His Philosophy

For him, philosophy must not be a thing aloof from everyday life but must be constantly applied to political, social, economic and educational problems. Dewey was greatly influenced by the doctrine of evolution and pragmatism in the 19th century. He studied evolution as applied in child study and pragmatism in its insistence on the subordination of intellect to practical ends. Pragmatism teaches that what is useful — what works in a practical situation — is true; what does not work is false. Truth, thus becomes not a fixed, eternal thing, but something that is subject to change. What is true to-day may be false tomorrow.

Essentially pragmatic, Dewey rejects the idea of world of absolutes and unchangeable truths. He said that there are no fixed beliefs. Our world is one of change, of uncertainty, where action, not contemplation, brings success in man's struggle. Knowledge enables man to direct the change. Knowing and doing are one. Mind and action are one and inseparable. He did not give action a higher place than knowledge. He does not think practice as superior to thought. On the other hand he thinks that thought and action are complementary. Only such thoughts as change the world are true, for truth and usefulness are identical. The ideal society is one in which everyone is engaged in thinking and doing which contributes to the common well being.

Pragmatism has enabled the science of education to assume that utility is the test of educational values and that the worth of an educational experience is measured by the degree to which it functions in meeting the actual life needs of the individual and of society. This rather than the disciplinary or transfer should be the value of the things we teach and our methods of teaching them. That is why Dewey talked about only those things which stood the test of experience.

He emphasized the importance of science and of scientific methods as central in the governing of human affairs of all kinds. In the scientific method, he found principles of procedure that gave him a conception of experience, knowledge and thinking. According to him knowledge and thinking are closely associated with action. And again knowledge and action are not separated into two opposing spheres. Ideas (knowledge) are not separate from action. They are tentative hypotheses or plans of action. They have to be tested by activity and by knowing the consequences of their being acted upon.

He said that thinking analyses the problem in four steps: (1) there is a sense of disturbance about the problem *i.e.* the problem or a difficulty comes before us, (2) then there is an observation of the conditions surrounding the problem, (3) formulation of hypothesis or plans of action, and (4) there is experimental testing which enables us to see whether the hypotheses or plans of action, when acted upon, give the desired result or not. Applying this process of thinking to education Dewey says: (1) the student should be the centre of experience and should be continuously engaged in activities in which he is interested. Then the problem would confront him as a genuine stimulus to thought; (2) he must possess or obtain the appropriate information for dealing with the problem; (3) then hypothesis or suggested solutions must occur to him and he should develop them in an orderly manner; (4) finally he should be given the opportunity to test his ideas by applying them in practice. Thus their meanings would become clear. He would discover for himself whether his ideas are true or not. By this Dewey wanted to prove that educational methods really consist in the method of thinking, made conscious and realised in action.

Thinking to him is personal and variable. It is influenced by human emotions and capacities. It was, therefore, according to him, not possible to establish any absolutes of truth and reality. Meaning of a concept depends on its relationship to the individual.

He was not concerned as much with the result of thought as with the process of thought. Through the process he said, the adjustment between a person and his environment is brought about. It is through modifying the environment or being modified by the environment that more growth or more development of human beings takes place. Thought, therefore, becomes an instrument, whereby the organism (human being) adjusts himself to its environment. The philosophy embodying this view is called instrumentalism and Dewey was an instrumentalist. Thought, he said, should have its bearing upon the solutions or practical problems. Since man is an organism, under the process of evolution, and adapting himself to a changing environment through mental processes, he ought to use his mental powers to solve the practical problems of his own preservation with reference to society.

It is in the course of putting ideas to the test of experience that education is gained. He wanted to give to his pupils wide opportunities for the practice and experience of purposeful enquiry. Experience was his great slogan. That's why he is called a great experimentalist. *His was an education of, by and for experience.*

John Dewey was convinced of the organic relationship between the individual and the society. He wants the individual not to commune with nature alone but with his fellow beings and to wonder and appreciate their achievements. The environment of an individual is both natural and human. He should value the one as much as the other. Self, he said, cannot grow in solitude. Nor can it grow in the mere contact with nature. For the growth of man the essential element is that he should live with the rest of mankind. This is a natural condition. "The make up of an individual includes reflections of a multitude of men; his thoughts are their thoughts". Just as the knowledge of the physical world had led the man to control the physical world to some extent, similarly the understanding of social-interrelationship would bring about an extension of human development.

Humanity, he said, is divided by innumerable barriers of language, of caste, of nationality, of colour, of religion etc. These barriers hold men in ignorance. They are the cause of the stagnation and they sometimes retard a nation. It is education, which, according to Dewey, can break down these barriers and forge links between individuals and groups. Then there would be no place for war in the integrated world. "The aim of living," says he, "is the ever enduring process of perfecting, maturing, refining."

His New Outlook of Psychology

The educational doctrines of John Dewey are rooted chiefly in his psychology, different from the old one. While his stress is placed upon the social aspects of education, he approached its problems psychologically. His concept of mind was much different when compared to the concept of mind of the old psychologist. He recognised the individual differences and took into consideration the impulses and interests of child when he expounded his theories of education.

Mind : Dewey was an evolutionist and instead of thinking mind as a fixed entity, he considered it an organism in the process of development, presenting different phases of capacity and interest at different periods. The older view was that mind is the same throughout, fitted with some faculties. Some faculties, such as memory came into play earlier while others like judgement and inference appeared later. The boy was assumed to be a little man and his mind a little mind in everything. Dewey did not believe in this. He said that mind is a product of activity and it develops through activity.

According to the faculty view of mind, the logically arranged principles and facts which are the subject matter of adult thought are the 'natural' studies of the child. Human knowledge is first sub-divided into sections, entitled as 'subjects'. Each subject then is broken up into parts. Some one part is assigned to a certain year of the school. No order of development is recognised, except that the earlier parts are easier than those that come later. Dewey rejected this thesis. He said that at first clear view should be taken of the dominant direction of activity at successive periods of life. This can be obtained through a scientific study of the learning mind. Then there should be a selection and grading of the material suitable for the course of study at each period by means of experience and experiment.

Old psychology was a psychology of intellect. Emotion and endeavour occupied an incidental place. Stress was laid on learning to think aright. According to the genetic view of mind — the view held by Dewey — thought arises from the need to meet some practical difficulty and is never an end in itself. In education action should have the primary place. Education is purposeful activity in the solution of problem recognised by pupils as worthwhile, and involving reflection as to means, ends, and consequence of one's actions. The activity must be inspired, not by the teacher, but by the pupil's own urge for a solution of a problem. It should arise freely and spontaneously out of life situation.

Individual differences : Dewey recognised the individual differences. But he was convinced that the individual grows through a richness of social opportunity. He has a faith that such opportunity for the realisation of human interdependence will encourage the will to do better and to be better. "The good man", says he, "is the man who no matter how morally unworthy he has been, is moving to become better."

Impulses and interests : Education, he said, should start by the capturing and focusing of natural impulses. Child's 'spontaneous attention' must be drawn to problems and topics which arouse his spirit of enquiry. The powers, thus aroused, should be developed and must also be controlled. Besides the natural impulses, will and reason also play their part in making decisions or in entering upon activities. This 'reflective attention' has also to be developed in the childhood.

Dewey said that organism has the capacity for active self-motion. It reaches out towards objects and experiences which should bring it to greater and richer life. In this process innate impulses do not lie passively, ready to be aroused by stimuli in the environment. On the other hand the organism explores the environment and picks out and reaches towards those environmental factors which offer him (the organism) the opportunities for self-expression, satisfaction and development.

This outward impulse, according to Dewey, is true interest. He defined interest as "a form of self-expressive activity — that is, of growth through acting upon nascent tendencies". Interest is 'an out-going of the self towards that which lies in the direction of the organisms development. He also said that stronger the interest, stronger will be the effort of will, which can be called to help to solve intervening difficulties and problems. He did not consider learning through interest as easy way of learning. He said that it was a way of calling into play the full powers of effort and determination of the learner. Interests are signs of growing powers. They require careful and constant observation. They should neither be excessively humoured nor excessively repressed. Repression weakens intellectual curiosity and kills initiative. Unguided humouring results in "transiency, caprice and whim." When the individual identifies himself with the fact to be learnt, then his interest is genuine. This is his moving or the driving force. Effort comes when the activity is confronted with obstacles. The effort to overcome obstacles stimulates thinking and reflection, which are the only really educative activities. Interest cannot be genuinely attached to a formal subject. It must be inherently contained in the activities in which the child engages himself. These activities may be physical, constructive, intellectual and social.

His Educational Theory

On such a philosophy and psychology, as outlined above, Dewey based his educational theories. Until the close of nineteenth century the religiously motivated moral aim, the disciplinary aim and informational aim ruled the educational world. Dewey was opposed to all these three aims of education. He re-stated the aims of education in the light of the rapid, social and economic changes.

Education, according to him, has two sides — the psychological and the social, neither of which can be subordinated or neglected.

Education is Psychological : The nature of the child is dynamic, reconstructing and reorganising. Education, therefore, should start with the psychological nature of the child. The teacher must utilise the activity springing from the nature and make it coincide with his efforts. The child should be put in the complete procession of all his powers, capacities, skills and judgement. This is possible only if teachers begin with an insight into the psychological interests and habits of the child, interpreting them in their usefulness as social instruments of action. Education is thus an active process of experiencing or rather a process of continuous re-formation of experience towards more significant social meaning.

Dewey insisted that constant experimentation to learn the child's nature should be undertaken so that school practices should be adapted to his effective development. Since the child is inherently active and bubbling over with the impulse to do, it is, therefore, the function of education to direct him properly. According to Dewey these impulses are of 4 kinds: (1) the social impulse of communication or conversation; (2) the constructing impulse to make things; (3) the impulse to investigate into things; and (4) the impulse of artistic or creative expression. These potentialities should be so developed that the child may be able to go beyond the stage of development reached by his predecessors. For such an achievement the school should change from listening basis to a doing basis. It must be arranged to enable the child to learn by experience and to think by managing experience. Mind as thinking or intelligence perceives and tests the meaning of behaviour or experience and controls environment. Dewey defined thinking as, "bringing the meanings of past experience to bear on the interpretation of new situation. The means of education, therefore, are play, construction, use of tools, contract with nature, expression and activity.

Social Efficiency : The aim of education, according to Dewey is social efficiency. He considered the school as a social institution, its processes not basically different from the social processes outside the school. The school is simply that form of social life in which all the factors are concentrated that will most effectively and rapidly bring the child to share in the accumulated knowledge and skill of the race. The school, therefore, should grow out of the home and play life which are the sources of child's principal experiences. The teacher must be familiar with the social situation. It would enable him to interpret properly the child's activities and transfer them into social channels. Education should proceed by the participation of the individual in social-relationships with his fellow human beings. Acquaintance with social institution and industrial processes takes place by actual living and working. The school is social environment, "simplified, purified, balanced and graded". Originality and initiative should be the chief virtues of the school life and then learning takes place.

In this shared life the teacher is a directing force, and organiser of the environments. The best moral training is received not in the form of dictates or discipline from the teacher but as the child is directed to meet the exigencies attendant on entering into proper social relationships with others in the school. The teacher, therefore, should not impose fiats or try to form rigid habits in child. He should select the proper influences to effect the child and assist him in responding to them.

John Dewey formulated 'social efficiency' as aim of education in view of the changed tenor of the society. This change has been brought by the application of science to the means of production and distribution, by the rise of great manufacturing centres and by the rapid growth of means of communications. The old family had broken down. Village community had disappeared. Habits of discipline and responsibility that were earlier formed in the family system of economy are no longer possible. The modem child, he pointed out, lived in a world of manufactured goods and had only a vague idea of how they came into being. The child never sees the cloth till he sees it in the form of clothes, nor food stuffs till they appear on the table. His house is illuminated by electricity that only needs a button to be pressed. The country child half a century ago, according to Dewey, was more fortunate in his daily experiences. He saw in the immediate neighbourhood of his own home all the processes of cloth making from the shearing of the sheep to the working of the loom. Instead of pressing a button for electric light, the whole process of getting illumination was followed in its toilsome length from the killing of the animal and trying of the fat to the making of wicks and the dipping of candles. His ordinary life, therefore, was of much greater educational work, both on the intellectual and the moral side, than that of the child of today. By sharing in the domestic duties the child built up mind and character, without any conscious effort. In fact the motives for learning were present in abundance in the daily routine. Since these activities were absent now, it became the duty of the school to enlarge the function of education.

Dewey believed the school to be a fundamental method of social progress and reform. Through education, society can formulate its own purposes, organise its means of attainment, and shape itself in the direction it wishes to go. This is the essence of democratic social order. The handling down of ready-made concepts is the mark of an autocratic social order. With the advance of social and political democracy, which requires change and progress, a new 'social education' is needed. This 'social education' Dewey held, should make effort to make vocational interests of any kind a means for promoting the common life. "A society is a mode of associated life characterised by the common purpose and activity of its members". Social environment consists of all the activities of fellow-beings that are bound up in the carrying on of the activities of any of its members. Democratic society makes provision for participation in its good of all its members on equal terms. It secures flexible readjustment of institutions through interaction of different forms of co-operative life.

When the psychological approach is isolated from the social, education produces either a barren and formal development of mental powers, with no idea of the use to which they are to be put, or it would be a forced and external education, resulting in subordinating the freedom of the individual to a pre-conceived notion of the society.

It is, therefore, essential that the school should include both the social and the individual goal. Social institutions do not give to man. They create him. Individuality is wrought out. Personality is achieved. Education is the means of social continuity and development of individuality. The place of individual in society depends upon native aptitudes, and not on wealth and social position. Social welfare depends upon man finding and filling his place in life.

Education is Life: Dewey believed that education is not a preparation for life. It is life. The school is a miniature society facing problems similar to those faced in life. Children should, therefore, be made participators in the social and moral struggles of their communities. Since they are to live in a democratic society, they should help to organise one and live in it. The basic purpose of the school is to train pupils in 'co-operative and mutually helpful living'. The child is to share the resources of a good society and to give back to that society, thus helping the development of other members. By give-and-take process the growth of the individual and the group is achieved. This should not be done by giving information but by varied experience. The more varied the experience, the better the society, for each member can develop more fully as an individual and then has more to give back to the group. The pupils confronting social problems shall create their own social order by solving the problems. The school should thus serve to free society from its inherited evils by identifying itself with social and democratic life.

Education should combine theory and practice : The aim of education, said Dewey, should, be to secure a balanced interaction of the practical and the theoretical attitudes. Some critics of John Dewey have blamed him for putting too much emphasis upon experience, action, and practice. But this is wrong. He always insisted that action and thought should go side by side. Practical side of a thing is very important but he said that it is a mistake to ignore the theoretical side which would emancipate the pupils from the limits of routine and customs. He said that those who have a taste for abstract topics should be provided ample opportunities for the concrete applications of ideas. Similarly individuals, with practical bent of mind, should be initiated into theory.

This combination of theory and practice in the school can be achieved through occupations. By occupation, Dewey does not mean any kind of busy work but activities like wood work, cookery, etc., which we have in social life. Such occupations have necessary balance of action and thought. Active self-expression takes place through the hands, eyes, continued observation, planning and reflection. In the background there is a whole wide range of intellectual, aesthetic and moral interest. By employing occupations systematically and by giving them a definite place in the school, healthy personal interest in learning is assured. This is the pre-condition of all real education. Children are interested in occupations. A great many of their own plays are simply miniature and haphazard attempts at reproducing series of occupations.

Education is Experience: Dewey's was an education by, of and for experience. He contended that the major developmental experiences of the human race have been gained in the struggle to satisfy needs. Natural impulse of human organism to seek food and protection has resulted in the evolution of human intelligence. It is through dominating impulses of the race that the development of the young child can be achieved. A conscious effort has to be made to make men more competent to take part in the activities and purposes of the race. This effort is education. Education, he said, helps, "the process of the reconstruction of experience, giving it a more socialised value through the medium of increased individual efficiency". Dewey points out that the achievement of the democratic way of life is singularly opportune for making this effort.

Other Aims of Education: Dewey attacked both the older attitude of formal indoctrination and the newer type of education, which attempted to train the individual for specific adult life. He agrees to the function of education as preparation for life, if it refers to life now and the immediate future. Pupils, he said, are not interested in the distant future. Any such attempt would not stimulate them to learn. The fostering of continuous healthy (that is successful) growth ensures adequate preparation for immediate life. This arouses the will of the pupil to venture further. Dewey also agreed with the aim of education as "self-realisation of the individual", if the teacher looks not into the distance at an imaginary product but to the present at a pupil *who exists, who grows, develops and achieves realisation of his powers all the time.* It is in the active development of the pupil that Dewey sees the place for individual education and the education of individuality. He wants each pupil's power and personality to be developed not according to any absolute standard but according to pupil's own capacities and opportunities. The pupils' progress is to be measured by his own best standard, and should not be set against those of other pupils who differ in natural ability, environmental experience and temperament. It is the duty of the teacher to observe individual desire and behaviour and should seek these tendencies to strengthen the process of growth. Education, he says, 'protects, sustains and directs growth'. Similarly Dewey would accept cultural aim as one of the aims of education so long as it allows a refining and guiding of personal taste rather than an imposition of arbitrary standard.

His Ideal School

According to Dewey the existing schools failed to keep pace with the changes that had occurred on account of Industrial Revolution and democratic set up of things, To bring the school into touch with real life was the basic aim of Dewey's experiment in Chicago when he set up a school in 1896, about which we have referred earlier.

Considering school as a psychological necessity he wanted ideal school like the ideal home. In the ideal home the parent is intelligent. He recognises what is best for his child and provides his needs. In the home the child learns by the daily conversations and by taking part in the household occupations. He learns the habits of industry, order and regard for the rights and ideas of others. The greatest virtue that is inculcated in the child at home is that he subordinates his interest to the general interest of the household.

Dewey considered ideal school as an enlarged ideal home. On account of better equipment and more scientific guidance, the discipline that the child learns at home, is continued in a more perfect form in the school. If the school is related to child's experiences, the child would have the same attitude towards it as he has towards the home. He would "find the same interest in going to school and in there doing things worth doing for their own sake, that he finds in the place and occupations which keep him busy in the home and neighbourhood life". The school, like the home, should be a genuine community engaged in common pursuits which interest the pupil and make him conscious that he is a contributing partner. On his efforts depends the success of the whole.

From his ideal school, traditions of bookishness have to be wiped out. Real life experiences of home and community have to be provided. Instead of a listening school it has to be an activity school, in which morals as well as occupational skills are acquired by living and acting in real situation. The economic, social, political and all other activities and problems of society should constitute the curriculum of the school. Through the school's various activities, the pupil's native impulses should be directed towards the reform of the society outside the school. No pre-conceived notions of society are to be imposed upon children. Moral education has to be given not by precepts but through activities performed jointly with others. The school must enable the child to attain his consciousness of the society.

Dewey not only stressed the occupations in his ideal school, but he also said that all the great human interests should be presented to the child in a developing sequence and in accordance with the stage of mental development of the child. He outlined a definite scheme of three stages of the elementary school *viz.*, (a) the play period from 4 to 8; (b) period of spontaneous attention from 8 to 12 and (c) period of reflective attention from 12 onwards.

In the first period the child begins to come out of the narrow limits of home life. He makes acquaintance with the social world. He cannot distinguish between means and ends. His first study is the life and occupations of the home and then start his larger social activities on which his home is dependent. Finally, he learns about the development of fundamental inventions and occupations. Reading and writing and geography are taught in the last year. In the period of spontaneous attention the child is able and willing to acquire different forms of skill. He understands the difference between means and ends. He can analyse the details and can act according to rules for the solution of practical problems. At this stage special studies have to be introduced. He has to be shown how human purposes have been achieved under various conditions.

The period of reflective attention comes when the child has sufficiently mastered the methods of thoughts, enquiry and activity. These should be appropriate to various aspects of experience so that the children may be able to specialise upon distinct studies and arts for technical and intellectual aims. The pupil at this stage is able to raise problems for himself and to seek solutions for them.

Dewey's Conception of Curriculum and His Methods

Since the main hypothesis of Dewey was life itself, in his curriculum he included the occupations and associations which serve the needs of man. He rejected the faculty view of mind. Therefore he did believe in a curriculum based upon fixed human knowledge, sub-divided logically into subjects, and parts of subjects, woven into courses capable of being completed in fixed intervals of time. Subjects, he said, are but summaries and re-capitulations of human activities. Therefore they should be reached by children summarising their own experiences. Subject compartments are not necessary to children. By giving too much importance to traditional subjects in the time table the pupils cannot be expected to delve into economics, or astronomy, or engineering or other important spheres in their search for solutions to their problems.

He saw the child as a unity developing through its own activity, but in a social setting. Mind he said, is essentially social. It was made what it is by society and depends for its development on a social environment. Earlier psychology regarded mind as a purely individual affair and was thought to be in direct contact within external world. Now the tendency is to conceive individual mind as a function of social life. It requires continual stimulus from social agencies. It finds its nutriment in social supplies. Social experience interprets for the child the meaning of physical world such as light, sound, heat etc. These have been transformed by man in accordance with his social needs and aims. It is, therefore, essential that social experience should form the main factors of curriculum.

Formerly when the mind was supposed to be in direct contact with the world, the requirements of instruction were that the child was brought into direct relations with various masses of external fact labelled as geography, arithmetic, grammar etc. It was not realised at that time that these studies had been born out of social situations and supplied answers to social needs. They were presented to the child as mere information. No attempt was made to relate them to his needs. Under the new psychology the subject matter of history, science and art are no longer foreign to the pupil's actual experiences. They are no longer empty-symbol having no meanings for him. Instruction is a "continual reconstruction, moving from the child's present experiences out into that .... which we call studies". Once the right connection between the child and curriculum is established in this way, there will be great motivation for learning: There is no necessity to make the memory do the work which should be done by reason. Action, said Dewey, must be given priority to abstract thought.

Since he rejected the ready-made curriculum he wants it to grow out of pupil's interests, impulses, and experiences and should consist of activities and projects leading to 'reconstruction of experience'. For this he said the fund of past human experience should be used. The teacher with his own greater experience and on account of knowing his pupils should help the children to select from that fund. He should also see, "what is there in the child's present that is usable with reference to it (past experience); how much elements are to be used; how his own (teacher's) knowledge of the subject matter may interpret the child's needs and doings, and determine the medium in which the child should be placed in order that the growth may be properly re-directed". This shows that the Deweyan teacher has to organise learning situations for pupils. It is necessary for him to plan ahead. The plan of the teacher should give balanced and coherent experiences to each pupil and at the same time foster the growth of group-consciousness. While emphasising the activities and occupations as forming the curriculum, he does not want that attempts should be made, "to arrange them in an order beginning with one having least worth and going on to that of maximum value. In so far as any study has a unique and irreplaceable function in experience, in so far as it marks a characteristic enrichment of life, its worth is intrinsic and incomparable. The only ultimate value which can be set up is just the process of living itself". Although this clearly shows that he indicated no order of preference for classifying human activities, he says that the curriculum "must be planned with reference to placing essentials first and refinements second". His essentials are man's fundamental concerns like food, shelter, clothing, household furnishings and the appliances connected with production, exchange and consumption". He made industrial activities, and their historical and social development, the centre of the curriculum and grouped the rest of the studies around this centre.

Aesthetic, moral and religious education was not omitted by Dewey from his curriculum. For full development, he considered Art as, "perfected expression of basic human activity." He writes, "viewed both psychologically and socially the arts represent not luxuries or superfluities, but fundamental forces of development." When the pupil solves his problems practically, it gives him wide opportunities for creative and appreciative activity in the arts and crafts. He develops a "wider understanding of artistic quality in industrial design and imaginative significance in more abstract art." Similarly he wants the moral and religious education to be an integral part of the basic experiences of the child. He hates those systems which claim to have character development as their main aim and yet in practice they do nothing to develop the character. He does not want to give religious and moral education through lessons but by practical experience. Purposeful activity and a curriculum comprising of 'standard factors of social life', in his opinion, would give the children moral interest and insight, "through the functioning of intelligence and will in the achievement of self-control and the appreciation of social values". Morality in discipline comes through the free and purposive judgement of the individual.

Dewey's methods of teaching comprised of three processes: (1) continuance of psychological order in the curriculum; (2) retention of problem method; (3) extension of social opportunity. The first is natural and therefore essential. The second would enable the pupils to learn "not so much things as the meaning of things". Social opportunities would arouse social consciousness, and essential factor for future citizens.

While the project or problem method entails co-operative effort, it is also possible, through this to correlate all the subjects necessary for the child to know. But Dewey warns the teacher not to allow projects "too ambitious and beyond the pupil's capacity to accomplish", as the children sometimes "exaggerate their powers of execution". For his problem or experimental method he laid down the following five steps, as essential: (1) the pupil should have a genuine situation of experience, *i.e.*, there should be a continuous activity in which he is interested for its own sake; (2) a genuine problem should arise from this situation and should stimulate the thinking of the child; (3) that he should possess or obtain information or make observation needed to deal with the problem; (4) the suggested solutions should occur to him; (5) he should have an opportunity to test his ideas by application, thus making their meaning clear and discovering for himself their validity.

Teacher in Dewey's Scheme

Dewey gave a very important role to the teacher. A Deweyan teacher should be concerned more with the pupil's impulses and interests rather than the inculcation of knowledge. His function is to guide the young through the complexities of life. For this he should provide them opportunities to learn in the natural way without facing frustration and injury. Frustration sometimes slows down and sometimes dams up the out-flowing of impulses towards greater and more abundant life. The teacher has not only to help the children to cope adequately with contemporary conditions, he should produce a race of young people, competent to cope with new experiences and new tasks which come before them. John Dewey gave great freedom to the child. But this freedom has to be regulated and organised by the teacher. The teacher, "as a stage manager is more powerful than the teacher as a player strutting and fretting". He may not have the plasticity to adopt his own personality to new growth, but since he is ahead of his pupils in experience, he should survey the social heritage and look to a more distance and purpose than his pupils. He should make a more reliable hypothesis as to the best course of action to pursue, because he has more experience of life. Competence of teachers should be judged by their skill in judging 'what will work'. The judge of this skill would be the society, which would see the quality of the product that the teacher gives to it.

The teacher, therefore, should realise his own power and responsibility to guide the young for the acquirement of the skill and knowledge which have raised man in the past. He must realise that his own superiority in experience and knowledge should enable the pupils to reach a stage higher than his own (teachers) in the evolutionary scale. The teacher must at the same time ensure that the individual and the group move in harmony, "both acquiring the best and most positive habits of growth".

Instead of wasting his time in 'chalk and talk' instruction and in the establishment of rigid discipline, the teacher must observe, plan and encourage. Self-discipline and group discipline develops through the will of the pupil themselves. But that does not mean that the Deweyan teacher is merely to follow the child wherever he leads. Professor Dewey's child-centred curriculum gave to teacher a heavier responsibility and a greater opportunity for guiding the young not only into the habit of democratic co-operation but also towards the highest intellectual pursuits and the fullest aesthetic experiences.

While Dewey prescribed the wider and wider range of experience for the child, he was conscious of the danger of fruitless repetition in some cases. He, therefore, wanted his teacher to indicate short cuts and to persuade the pupil to engage in progressive activities. For this, must he know the intelligence and temperament of each pupil.

Comparison with other Educators

Dewey's principles of social co-operation and expression 'of individual activities are in accord with the work of Froebel. But Dewey went a step further. Instead of having stereotyped 'gifts' and 'occupations', Dewey's activities were more expressive of real life. In carrying on these activities Dewey insisted that the child should be given "whenever possible, intellectual responsibility for selecting the materials and instruments that are most fit, and given an opportunity to think out his own model and plan of work, lead to perceive his own errors and find how to correct them." The children were introduced into the complexities of contemporary life through simplified experiences and terms they could understand. They learned to do by doing, rather than by listening. They were prepared for social efficiency and participation in a democratic society not by mere passive obedience but by acquiring the necessary social insight and initiative and meeting the responsibilities of that society. Both Froebel and Dewey agree that education is growth. But while Froebel wants the individual to realise the Absolutes, for Dewey there are no Absolutes.

Rousseau had emphasised the importance of child's nature and minimised environment. But Dewey believed that neither the psychological nature of the individual nor the social environment of the culture could be slighted. He said that a democratic society could be attained only by the proper interaction of the two.

Dewey rejects Froebel's symbolism. For the symbols he would substitute real life experiences and occupations and thus is the exponent of pragmatism.

His Contribution

John Dewey's most philosophic and practical mind made far reaching contributions to the curriculum and methods of teaching. The beliefs of this psychologist and thinker par excellence emerged from his teaching experience and his own environment. That is why his was an education of, by, and for experience.

The experiment in education developed by Dewey at Chicago in 1896 in this experimental school has stimulated the effort to bring the school into intimate relation to the community life. His ideas on the practice of education were in touch with the actualities of life. The activity movement, directed towards the problem of social life, has made wide advances not only in the growth of school embodying its philosophy but in stimulating educational reform in existing institutions of every grade. The activists stress social rather than intellectual activism. They have agreed that pupil's activity, whether spontaneous or directed, is the best method of learning.

Experimental schools in the present day are due to Professor Dewey. In these schools new use of education can be put to the test of experience and developed in accordance with the results actually obtained in practice.

In emphasising the importance of the interests of the child, Dewey made another contribution to the enrichment of education. The schools are endeavouring to apply a new conception of the nature of the children and of the learning process to education.

The fusion of psychological and sociological aspects of education is the greatest contribution that Dewey made to educational thought. He told that school should foster a community life, a process of living where the complexities of social life are "simplified, purified and balanced." The school must provide activities in which relations with others are prominent. The teacher, said Dewey, is the senior member of the school community rather than an officer appointed to impose certain ideas.

Dewey in reconciling the supposedly opposed doctrines of interest and effort, proved that effort can be summoned only by connecting an activity with some end in which the child has an interest.

Dewey's analysis of effective thinking called attention to the importance of the 'problem to stimulate thinking.' It stressed the need to locate and define the difficulty, to examine the suggestions and possible solutions, to develop the bearing of each and finally to submit the solution to the test of application. This analysis paved the way for the so-called problem method of teaching or the project method of teaching.

Project method is the practical outcome of Dewey's philosophy. It is employed by educationists in all countries. The method translates the idea of education through occupations into a form suitable for the ordinary school. Instead of learning lessons from the teacher, the pupils are faced with some task to be accomplished, some problem to be solved. If the project is suited to the age and experience of the children, the interest it creates, carries them beyond the immediate activity into a varied learning.

Dewey drew principally upon the growing forces of democracy, science, industrialism, evolution and pragmatism for support. Few aspects of life and thought have remained beyond the range of his investigation. He has surveyed such realms of thought and human activity as aesthetics, politics, ethics, logic, religion, and education, and has made a notable contribution to the thought in all the fields which he has touched.

This is a complex world. A struggle for stability is going on. In this world awareness of individual responsibility must be aroused. It is the school which can contribute by training the young in specific and experimental thinking and by helping them to experience the need for democratic co-operation. This was Dewey's great message for school and society. He saw human progress as dependent upon the opening up of lines of communication between pupils, nations, classes and all smaller groups. The attainment of social unity was his goal. In the words of Bertrand Russel, Dewey has an outlook which, "is in harmony with the age of industrialism and collective enterprise" and in the words of another writer, "the Deweyan revolution in education, we see, has already carried us a long way."

6

Rabindranath Tagore

(1861—1941)

There is no death for Rabindranath Tagore. He is immortal in our history and his writings will fill our hearts for all times to come.

— Dr. S. Radhakrishnan

In the firmament of education two master-minds of India will remain outstanding — Rabindranath Tagore and Mahatma Gandhi. Unlike most of the Western educators they were not only theorists but practitioners. Their results are epitomized in Shantiniketan and basic education. Both of them discovered the fundamental unities of our culture. They brought our people together on the binding basis of all that is essential in our civilization and then showed the right path not only to Indians but also to the world. They offered to humanity the deepest and divinest in India's cultural heritage with unflinching faith in the spiritual unity of man.

His Life

Rabindranath Tagore was born in Calcutta on May 6th, 1861. He had his first lessons from a private tutor at home. But he writes, "It was no one's fault but my own, that nothing could keep me for many days together in the beaten track of learning. I strayed at will, filling my wallet with whatever gleanings of knowledge I chanced upon." He had plenty of opportunity for education at home, where he was taught physiology, language, mathematics and Sanskrit. By nature he loved beauty, music and poetry. Later he was admitted into a school but he did not like it and his father arranged for his studies at home. In order to enable him to learn enough mastery of spoken English, he was admitted into Bengal Academy. When he had grown a little older he was sent to St. Xavier's School, Calcutta, but there, too, he felt unhappy. His teachers pronounced that he was unfit for studies. One of his teachers, however, found means of keeping him occupied. He gave him the whole of Kumarsambhav to learn by heart. He shut him in a room and gave him Macbeth to translate. By setting him free, in this way, from the fixed curriculum they reaped some rewards for their labours. But his resolute refusal to be educated stood proofs against authority and blandishment and he was allowed to continue his studies at home. He himself says, "some people get hammered into shape in the book-learning factories, and these are considered in the market to be goods of a superior stamp...it was my fortune to escape almost entirely the impress of these mills of learning. The Masters and Pandits who were charged with my education soon abandoned the thankless task......(his teacher) realised that this boy could never be driven along the beaten track of learning".

At the age of 16 Tagore was sent to England with his brother to study law. But this subject did not appeal to him and he returned to India after one year. That he did not become a Barrister while in England, never gave him the shock. During this stay, however, he developed a good taste in English literature by joining the London University, though for three months only. By coming into personal contacts, his understanding of human nature developed side by side with his knowledge of literature.

On reaching back in India he began to produce a new type of literature and became a very important figure. His first collection of poems, entitled "Songs of the Morning" was published when he was twenty.

Although Rabindranath Tagore did not attend the traditional school for long, he did not altogether escape from its molestation. The short period for which he attended the traditional school was sufficient to give him the knowledge of how our children suffer. Such a school appeared to him stiff, cramping and dead. A realisation at this stage helped him to formulate his own philosophy of life and ideal of education.

It was at the age of 40 that he started a school of his own in Bengal. Fortunately the place for such a school was ready to his hands. His father had selected a lonely spot for his life of communion with God. This place, with permanent endowment, he dedicated to the use of those who sought peace and seclusion for their meditation and prayer. Here came Tagore with 10 boys and started a new life and new work. In this school he gave a name and local habitation to his dynamic idealism. This school known as Shantiniketan Ashram, became in 1921 the world famous Vishwabharati — a seat of international University seeking to develop a basis on which the culture of East and West may meet in common fellowship.

The University has been growing up for over 35 years, passing through many vicissitudes. There was a time when the British bureaucracy looked at it with suspicion. There were many stages when scantiness of resources stared the poet into his face. But reliance upon truth rather than upon material helped it to grow stronger and stronger day-by-day.

In 1909 his world famous work 'Gitanjali' was published and he went to England in 1912 with it. The Irish poet W.B. Yeats spoke very highly of the value and quality of this "work of supreme culture". Next year he was awarded the Nobel Prize for Literature. The Calcutta University and the Oxford University honoured him by conferring on him the honorary degrees of doctorate. The Government made him the "Knight though this title the poet renounced in 1919 as a protest against the Amritsar Massacre that year.

Rabindranath Tagore was not fortunate in his family life. His wife died in 1902. Very shortly after her death his daughter died of consumption. Then his youngest son died of cholera. But these deaths did not break his heart and he continued his great mission of life — educating people in the lap of nature. Besides visiting England thrice, he visited America, Russia and many other countries of Europe and Asia. It was in 1941 that he fell ill and died on the 7th August.

His Philosophy

Like Rousseau, Tagore was an 'individualist' and 'naturalist'. He believed in the right and freedom of the individual to shape his life in his own way. But in the individual's development he ultimately wanted the unity of mankind. He said that every individual is different from another and everyone is unique. In everyone of us the Creator manifests in a unique, though imperfect manner and every individual tries to realise the Creator in his own way. In the Creator and through Him we find unity not only amongst human beings but also between man and nature.

That great lover of nature gave a very important place to Nature. This, he said, is the manifestation of the Creator (Brahman). Through its various forms, colours and the rhythms the Brahman reveals himself through many ways. He reveals Himself more clearly through nature than through man. Tagore, therefore, wished human beings to have a close communion with nature and with its purifying and vitalising influences. Just as a man realises his relationship with human beings, he should realise his relationship with the nature.

"Experience of the spiritual world, religion as the right centre of life's activities and the unity of thought and truth" was the keynote of Tagore's great philosophy. There should be spiritual relationship between man and man. This will knit human beings into communities. Tagore's individualism, therefore, is compatible with the growth of social units. He encouraged the individual to reorganise the social groups on the basis of the individual's spiritual worth. By that he never meant parochialism — intellectual, social, political and spiritual. He wanted the essential unity of the universe. True, that he advocated internationalism but not economic or political internationalism. He wanted the spiritual bondage of the universe. Having faith in the fundamental unity of mankind he preached human brotherhood.

Like the ancient sages and seers, Tagore emphasised that the aim of life should be to be prepared for the other world. He wanted man, to "have access to the life that goes beyond death and rises above all circumstances." His advice was "let us find our God, let us live for the ultimate truth which emancipates us from the bondage of the dust and gives us the wealth, not of things but of inner light, not of power but of love."

His Educational Philosophy

His philosophy of education conforms to his general philosophy. He approached education as he approached life as a poet, with a totality of vision. He was fully aware of education's innumerable implications. "Education", he said, "is a permanent part of the adventure of life,......it is not like a painful hospital treatment for curing them (students) of the congenial malady of their ignorance, but is a function of the health, the natural expression of their mind's vitality." To him the object of education is freedom of mind through the path of freedom, though it had has its risk and responsibility too. Most people, he said, had forgotten that children were living beings. They were more living than grown up people, who had built their shells of habit around them, while the children are always pliable. Therefore, he wanted that children should not have mere schools for their lessons, but a world whose guiding spirit is personal love. "Love and action" he believed, "are the only mediums through which perfect knowledge can be obtained."

The three cordial principles of his educational philosophy are (1) Freedom, (2) Creative self-expression, (3) Active communion with nature and man. The genesis of the ideal of freedom lies in his own experience as a child and his experience of the prevailing system of education. About his early education he remarked "we had to sit like dead specimens of some museum whilst lessons were pelted at us from above like hail-storm on flowers". He spoke of the existing schools as being an "education factory, lifeless, colourless, dissociated from the context of the universe within the bare white walls staring like eye balls of the dead." Our education has taken us from our natural surroundings. It has weaned us from nature and its vitalising and life giving influences. It is dissociated from social contexts. An education "divorced from the streams of life and confined within the four walls of the class-room becomes artificial and loses its value." The first and the foremost work, in his opinion, was to bring the child's mind in contact with nature. Let the child imbibe and learn freely and spontaneously from the book of nature. Let him be happy and free. Education should be natural in content and quality. Through contact with nature the child will be introduced to the great world of reality easily and joyfully.

Education Naturalised

No educationist has felt more deeply and constantly the fascination of the great spaces of earth and sky, the boundless horizon and white lights of evening and the expanse of moonlight as Tagore felt and enjoyed. Like Rousseau he was also fond of Robinson Crusoe, where "man is face to face with solitary Nature, coaxing her, co-operating with her, exploiting her secrets, using all his faculties to win her help." His nature was attuned to ramblings in the open air. Such surroundings, he believed, nourished the child's nature spontaneously. Nature inspires the human beings differently at different stages of human development. "For the young child, Nature will become an unconscious symbol of superpersonal growth and evolution, something that need not be questioned and which provides an ever-ready background for its dreams and its play. For the adolescents, Nature will become an object of either scientific or lyrical curiosity. The adult will see in her the soil on which his country and his people grow, the cultural and economic background of human existence". Nature to him was the focus where the interests and aspirations of human beings meet. It is, therefore, essential riot only to know Nature but to live Nature. By this the man will attain the greater and deeper freedom. He will find fulfilment in the struggle from the dim dreamlands of childhood towards the light of maturity.

For education, he said, there should be a place where men have gathered for the highest end of life — in the peace of Nature, where life is not merely meditative but full in its activities; where men aspire to realise man's world as God's kingdom; they must aspire to be the citizens of that world. It should be a place where the sunrise and a sun-set and the silent glory of stars are not daily ignored; where Nature's festivities of flowers and fruits have their joyous recognition from men. It should be such a place where the young and the old, the teacher and the students sit at the same table to partake of their daily food and the food of their eternal life. Tagore said that we have come to this world to accept it, not merely to know it. The highest education is that which does not merely give information but makes our life in harmony with all existence. Unfortunately such education is ignored in our traditional schools. From our childhood habits are formed and knowledge is imparted in such a manner that our life is weaned away from nature. Our mind and world are set in opposition from the beginning of our days. Convinced of these ideals, he set all his resources to create such an atmosphere. He founded a school, which was not imposed upon the boys by autocratic authorities. It was impressed upon their minds that it was their own world, upon which their life should fully and freely react. Freedom of mind, heart and will are the governing features of Tagore's institution — The Shantiniketan.

He wanted an equilibrium of the 'Natural' and the 'Civilised' forces in man. The art of education according to him, should consist in training the child to inhibit all those impulses that are anti-social. "For our perfection we have to be vitally savage and mentally civilised; we should have the gift to be natural with nature and human with human society". It was, why, he suggested that besides communion with nature, there should be communion of man with man. This would enable them to learn social behaviour and co-operation in educational activities.

Education, in the academic sense of mere acquisition of knowledge or information never appealed to the comprehensive genius of the poet. Education to be real must be of the whole man, of his emotions and senses as much as of his intellect. One finds, therefore, that from the very beginning Shantiniketan gave a prominent place to art. Among other subjects learnt in the open air under the shade of trees they had their music and picture making. The 'Kalabhawan' or the 'School of Fine Arts and Crafts' has developed into a well-known centre of Indian Art. Similarly dramatics and dancing got the rightful place in his scheme of education. A large part of man, he believed, can never find its expression in the mere language of words. It must have many other languages — lines and colours, sounds and movements for the satisfaction of his aesthetic urge. The poet regarded the language of sounds and movements to be the highest means of self-expression. Side by side with this provision for creative self-expression, he laid great stress on various forms of handwork. He said, "however great a scholar may be, if he has not educated his body, he has to live a life of dependence on others — in many ways he is an incomplete man. There is a close and inseparable connection between the faculties of mind and body. Each gains strength by co-operating with the other. If the education of the body does not proceed along with the education of the mind, the latter cannot gather strength". In his Ashram the effort was made for the education of the mind and all the senses through various activities. There, every pupil is taught to master some form of hand work or the other. "Hand work, music and arts", he said, "are the spontaneous overflow of our deeper nature and spiritual significance."

His Emphasis on Spiritual Education

For the harmonious development of the child the poet put great emphasis on the spiritual side along with the intellectual and physical side. The traditional schools put entire emphasis on the intellectual and the physical side of the man. They devoted their sole attention to giving children information, not knowing that they were, by this emphasis, accentuating a break between the intellectual, physical and the spiritual life. Experience of the spiritual world, whose reality we miss by our incessant habit of ignoring it from childhood, has to be gained by children by living in it and not through the medium of religious instruction. Teaching of religion, Tagore said, can never be imparted in the form of lessons. It is there where there is religion in living. Religion is not a fractional thing that can be doled out in fixed weekly or daily measures as one among various subjects in the school curriculum. It is the truth of our complete being, the consciousness of our personal relationship with the infinite. It is the true centre of gravity of our life. This can be attained during our childhood by daily living in a place where the truth of the spiritual world is not obscured by artificial necessities; where life is simple, surrounded by fullness of leisure, by ample space and pure air and profound peace of nature; and where men live with a perfect faith in the eternal life before them. Pointing out the importance of teaching of religion he remarked that religion establishes the right centre for life's activities, giving them eternal meaning. It maintains the true standard of value for the objects of our going higher and higher. It inspires in us the spirit of renunciation which is the spirit of humanity.

His Love for, and Methods with, Children

Profound was Tagore's love for children. He recognised the potentialities of childhood and wanted them to be happy and to be trained to use to the full their gifts of mind and body and spirit. What he hated was imprisonment of city life and class-room. For the children he longed for the freedom of the kite as it soars into the mid-day sky alone. Children, he said, are lovers of the dust. Their body and mind thirst for sun-light and air as flowers do. Their active sub-conscious mind, like the tree, has the power to gather food from surrounding atmosphere. For them the atmosphere is more important than rules and methods, buildings and appliances, class teaching and text books. They welcome direct communication with the universe through their senses. Childhood should, therefore, be given its full measure of life's draught. The young mind should be given an idea that it had been born in a human world, which is in harmony with the world around it. This is what our traditional schools ignore. They forcibly snatch away children from a world full of the mystery of God's own handiwork, *i.e.*, Nature. Traditional schools, he realised offered maimed opportunities. He saw that in the progressive countries the range of the life of children was varied and wide enough to give them necessary freedom for the development of their power.

Tagore never liked the school master moulding the child's mind according to his ready-made doctrines. "The schoolmaster", he said, "is of opinion that the best means of educating the child is by concentrating of mind, but mother nature knows that the best way is by dispersion of mind." Children, he believed, gather facts by scattering of mental energy and through unexpected surprises. Facts, therefore, should come first to children to startle their mind into full activity. He was conscious of child's fanciful activities and advocated that there should be a gradual transition from playful to purposeful activities.

The first important lesson for children would be that of improvisation. They should be provided constant opportunities to explore their capacities through surprises of achievement. Nothing ready-made should be imposed upon them. Their life should be creative. Only that teacher can teach them who has been learning himself. One who has lost the child in himself is absolutely unfit for the great work of educating children. It is not the subjects of study, organisation and equipment in the school that is important, but the living contact between the mind of the teacher and the mind of the taught that is important. It is then that real joy is born. It is then that the Guru can give in abundance and the pupil can take in abundance: Shantiniketan is supreme in establishing this living contact between the teacher and the taught.

A Great Practitioner

The fulfilment of all these theories and concepts in practice found expression in the various directions. Rabindranath was not a dreamer only to leave behind a legacy of mere ideas and ideals. He worked them out in the most constructive way. He created Shantiniketan which realised his educational ideals. He succeeded in making the inmates of the Ashrama forget that they were mere drudges, labouring day and night at their appointed tasks.

Shantiniketan is an abode of peace, where the young and the old, the teacher and the learner share the joys and the sorrows of life in a spirit of perfect comradeship. There he wanted teachers imbued with the feeling that they were there because of their own innermost need and not because of their ambition for doing good to others. The quality of the lessons, the perfection of method, the knowledge of subjects is important, but what is great deal more important is that there should be no consciousness of self importance.

Shantiniketan is an organism, not an organisation. It is not an educational factory producing ready-made boys and girls for consumption in society. It has not grown according to a well conceived plan. It has grown according to its own inner logic and that is the unique thing about it. Originating with ten boys in 1901, now students come in great number from far and near, live a common community life, dining in the same halls, playing on the same ground, organising common socials, picnics, excursions, literary and musical activities. In one place has been created an atmosphere of life lived in community and human fellowship and in constant awareness of the great living nature.

Tagore's 'Path Bhavan' is a progressive school imparting elementary and secondary education to children from 6 to 16 years of age. The school places emphasis not so much on a mere acquisition of knowledge as on a full and harmonious development of the child. The ideal of education through sharing a life of high aspiration with one's teacher took possession of his mind. Close personal contact with the teacher, the deep influence of nature and environment, the atmosphere of freedom and joy, the practical training given in co-operation and self-government, the effort made to develop the self-expressive side of the child mind through social, literary, artistic, musical and craft activities are some of the special features of the school. The surroundings there are filled with creative possibilities, with opportunities for the joy of play that is work — the work of exploration; and of work that is play. There is provided a succession of novel experiences.

Shantiniketan is a self-governing Republic. The boys have everything that is not luxury, their own dairy farm, their own post office, hospital and workshop. The boys go out to the villages to run night schools for the labouring classes and the lower castes. In this way caste exclusiveness is broken down in early years and the boys learn to work for their land. They hold their own courts.

Systematic arrangements now exist for advanced studies in Buddhist literature; Vedic and classical Sanskrit, Pali, Prakrit, Tibetan and Chinese. In order to bring the students and teachers of that University into close touch with the daily life of the common people, the Institute of Rural Reconstruction was founded in 1922. The Cheena Bhavana, the Hindi Bhavana, the School for studies in Islamic Culture are other institutions comprising the educational endeavour that Shantiniketan represents.

It is now a University — known in the world as Vishvabharati. In the ideals of Vishvabharati the poet sought to establish a relationship between East and West, to promote inter-cultural and inter-racial amity and understanding and fulfil the highest mission of the present age that is the unification of mankind.

Tagore had a benevolent object to perform. His was the ideal that human personality should be developed in an atmosphere of freedom and fellowship, through impulses of life, lived in nature and in close touch with varied creative activities of the human mind. There (Shantiniketan) prevails the atmosphere of Nature's own beauty with her varied gifts of colours and dance, flowers and fruits, with the joy of her mornings and the peace of her starry nights.

7

Mahatma Gandhi

(1869—1948)

Primarily a politician, statesman and social reformer, Mahatma Gandhi had made no less a substantial and solid contribution to the educational thought and practice in India. His life and career is so rich that volumes will be required to give a complete and full idea of his life's mission. We will therefore, touch in the following paragraphs those phases of life, which have helped him to have educational experience.

Mohandass Karamchand Gandhi was born at Porbander, Kathiawar, Western India, on October 2nd, 1869. He was sent to a local high school but as a student he was slow, shy and hesitant. His observance, however, of truth was real and continuous.

At 18 Gandhiji matriculated at Ahmedabad. A family friend persuaded his mother and elder brother to send him to England for the study of Law. His mother consented with much hesitation and he sailed for England on the 4th September, 1887. After studying for 4 years, he was called to the Bar on 10th June, 1891 and sailed back home.

He started his practice in Bombay but failed and returned to his native place, Rajkot. Here he received an offer from an Indian firm, which had a branch in South Africa, to go to that country to help them in an important case. In April, 1893, he sailed for Durban. Although his case was over, he continued to stay in Africa for 20 years. It was there that he saw a series of insulting events of disgracing Indians and his political feelings were awakened. He founded the Natal Indian Congress in 1894.

In 1903 he shifted to Transvaal. Like Pestalozzi at Yverdon and Burgdorf, Mahatma Gandhi had educational experiences on the Tolstoy Farm. On the Farm he undertook the responsibility of educating his own sons and other children. Like Rousseau and Pestalozzi he came to believe that, "true education could be imparted by the parents, and that there should be the minimum outside help."

Tolstoy Farm was just like a family, where Gandhiji occupied the place of the father. He helped the children in all round development. Training of heart and building of character received his first attention. These pupils had to devote 8 hours a day for vocational training and only 2 hours to book learning. The vocations taught were digging, cooking, scavenging, sandel-making, simple carpentry and messenger work. Since there were no servants on the Farm all work was done by the inmates. Besides teaching them the dignity of labour, they were helped to build their physique through manual work and no further games or exercise for that were required.

The ages of the children ranged from 6 to 16. They were very happy in learning by doing and in learning by co-operation. Although English was taught to them yet instruction in other subjects was given to them in their mother tongue. Their curriculum included Hindi, Tamil, Gujarati, Urdu, a little of Sanskrit, elementary History, Geography and Arithmetic. Mahatma Gandhi never used any text books. He taught them by word of mouth. That was more interesting and kept the children active as they were stimulated to put questions. Character building was inculcated by example of the virtuous life of the teacher rather than by the precept from the teacher. No corporal punishment was given to them even in cases of misconduct. The creed of non-violence, thus, was put into actual practice. Gandhiji was convinced that, "if good children are taught together with bad ones and thrown into their company, they will lose nothing, provided all of them were put under the watchful care of their parents and guardians."

In January, 1915, Gandhiji returned to India and the educational experiments tried in Africa were further continued for a short time at Shantiniketan and then at Sabarmati and Sewagram, where Gandhiji established his own Ashrams successively. Immediately on his arrival in India, Gandhiji along with the other members who had returned from Africa with him, repaired to Shantiniketan.

There he taught the inmates the great lesson of 'self help' by asking them to dispense with the cooks and do the cooking themselves. His stay, however, was very short and in May, 1915, he founded the Sabarmati Ashram. Beginning with 20 inmates, it grew into a patriarchal family, which had grown up around its spiritual father — Bapu — a name of endearment given to Gandhiji. There were women and children among the inmates. A school for children and illiterate adults was attached to the Ashram. There were gardens to till and beasts to tend, while every one performed his obligatory task at the spinning wheel. Every work of daily routine was done by the inmates. It was a village which prayed and worked and ate in common. The Ashram was a retreat to which men came for teaching and inspiration, spending a formative time under Gandhiji's guidance, that they might go out, fired with his spirit, to work for India. In the evening the inmates of the Ashram assembled for prayer. Discussions were held about the content, curricula and method of education in the school there. Gandhiji wanted to make that school a model for others to copy. Wardha scheme which came two decades later was the outcome of the experiments at Tolstoy Farm, Sabarmati Ashram and Sewagram.

The inmates of the Sabarmati Ashram had to observe many vows, for example: (1) Truth speaking; (2) Non-violence or Ahimsa; (3) Celebacy; (4) Control of palate; (5) Non-thieving; (6) Non-attachment or non-possession; and (7) Poverty. Then there were certain rules to be observed. For example, only swadeshi article could be used. Every one had to wear khaddar which was home spun and home woven. A spirit of fearlessness was inculcated among the inmates. Gandhiji believed that Indians were in the grip of paralysing fear. They feared their neighbours, their caste, their social superiors and their officials. This, Gandhiji, wanted them to rid of. Every Ashramite had to take a vow to end untouchability. Learning of as many vernaculars as possible was the rule of the Ashram.

In April, 1935, Gandhiji founded the Sewagram Ashram, 11 miles from Wardha. This new settlement was developed from scratch and for the next decade Gandhiji fought his battle for freedom of India from this place. It was here that he conceived the idea of his new system of education. Not only did he expound the Wardha scheme or the basic education, a practical shape was also given to the scheme in 1937.

His struggle for freedom of India was at last crowned with success in August, 1947, when India got independence. Ahead of him lay the great work of building New India, but a frenzied youth shot him down on the 30th January, 1948, and deprived not only India of a master-maker but also deprived the world of an apostle of peace and non-violence.

His General Philosophy

Mahatma Gandhi, the great thinker and experimenter, formulated his own views about everything in the world. Although he expressed his ideas on everything from God to birth-control, for our purposes his belief in God, Truth, Ahimsa and dignity of labour are most important. On the bases of these Gandhiji wanted to recreate an ideal spiritual society.

He had a profound faith in one God and believed in the unity of man. All that moves in the world, according to him, is due to God. Like Froebel he believed God as the Ultimate Reality "behind the universe which is always in a state of flux". While all other things, he said, are subject to change, God is "changeless, that holds all together, that creates, dissolves and recreates". God is benevolent as Gandhiji saw "that in the midst of death, life persists, in the midst of untruth, truth persists, in the midst of darkness light persists". To him God was "Life, Truth, Light and Love". Not only did he believe in the absolute oneness of God, he also believed in the oneness of humanity. He remarked, "What though we have different bodies? We have but one soul. The rays of the sun are many through refraction. But they have the same source. I cannot, therefore, detach myself from the wickedest soul, nor may I be denied identity with the most virtuous.......if we are the sons of the same God and partake of the same divine essence, we must partake of the sin of every person, whether he belongs to us or another race".

According to him God is "indefinable, mysterious power that pervades everything.. His (God's) presence is proved not by extraneous evidence but in the transformed conduct and character of those who have felt the real presence of God within." He, therefore, advised to "have a living faith in a living God who is the ultimate arbiter of our fate". His will is supreme. Gandhiji said, "All life in its essence is one and that men are working consciously or unconsciously towards the realization of that identity."

Until 1931 he said, “God is Truth”. But thence he said, “Truth is God”. For, he remarked, “denial of God we have known. Denial of Truth we have not known. The most ignorant among men have some truth in them. We are sparks of truth. The sum total of those sparks is indescribable, as yet unknown Truth”. Truth is an inner voice. It is the call of conscience. His advice was to realise that ‘Truth is life’. Not only he wanted to realise Truth himself, he wanted everyone to be a seeker of Truth. It was not scientific Truth that Gandhiji valued so highly, but social truth in all our dealings with our neighbours. He insisted on complete frankness in daily intercourse and condemned the insincerities practised in the name of politeness.

Gandhiji said that we must say “yes” only when we mean ‘yes’, and we must say ‘no’ when we mean ‘no’, regardless of the consequences. There should be harmony, he held, between thought, word and action. To think one thing, to speak another and do a third is untruth. “To mean 'no’ and say ‘yes’, to give word and not to keep it, to nurse ill-will in the mind and utter honied words to flatter a man at his face and malign him behind his back, to be fasting outwardly and think all the while of prospective rich fare, to consider a thing to be reprehensible and yet do it, are all examples of disharmony in thought, word and deed and therefore of untruth. This disharmony breaks up man’s personality and leaves him no peace of mind or happiness”. He repeatedly advised people to appear as they are. The naturalness was, in his view, a part of truthfulness. Devotion to truth at all costs was a passion with him throughout his life.

The means to attain the goal of Truth, suggested by Mahatma Gandhi, is Ahimsa or Non-violence. To him “Ahimsa and Truth are so intertwined that it is practically impossible to disentangle and separate them. They are the two sides of a coin, or rather a smooth metallic disc”, where it is nor possible to say “which is the obverse and which is the reverse?” It was, therefore, advised that ‘Truth being our goal, Ahimsa should be our supreme duty’ to achieve that goal. Ahimsa enjoins first of all, charity towards those who consider themselves our enemies. A person believing in Ahimsa or love must rise above attachment and hatred, fear and vanity. Patience, forbearance, humility, charity and readiness for compromise are also covered by the term non-violence. A non-violent person must live a life of Tapasya or austere living. Such a life would purify the spirit. The importance of spiritualism and morality should be recognised and all evils will be overcome through non-violence. This Ahimsa, Gandhiji declared, should be practised by individuals, groups, communities and nations. This is a great power which must be accepted as the law of life, must pervade the whole being and not be applied to isolated acts". Instead of being a "negative attitude, it is a 'positive and dynamic' quality. Satyagraha resists evil through law". It is a belief in the power of the spirit, the power of the truth, the power of love by which we can overcome evil through self- suffering and self-sacrifice.

Like Rousseau he wanted to recreate the society. He aimed at universal brotherhood, freedom, justice and equality for all. Exploitation of any kind and on any score was alien to him. Establishment of classless society was his greatest dream. Artificial barriers of caste, creed, colour, wealth and power were hated by him. It is a classless society, which according to him could realise the Absolute (God). He agreed with Tagore that individual development could take place in a spiritual society. The chief characteristic of such a society should be love, non-violence, truth and justice. "Moral force and moral sanction" would be the guiding factors of such a society.

In order to avoid the accumulation of wealth in a few hands, he proposed an economic and social structure which should be built upon the decentralisation of industrial agriculture. This decentralisation, he said, is possible if we encourage cottage and village industry. He, however, conceded the right to everyone to keep as much for himself as was "necessary for a refined, civilized and moral life."

In this society, service to God and community was the greatest of creed of Mahatma Gandhi. According to him , "man's ultimate aim is the realisation of God". All the activities — social, political, religious — of man, therefore, should be motivated by this one aim. We love and serve God when we love and serve His creatures. Service of all, therefore, should be the first fundamental of every human being. God, said Gandhiji, instead of being in the temple, church and mosque, is to be found in the "temple of humanity" and remarked that "man becomes great exactly in the degree in which he works for the welfare of his fellow men". In a society where the ideal is 'service unto all' there cannot be domination and exploitation of any kind. Moral and equitable principle would help that society to realise God, Who is Truth. Ahimsa or love would be the means of achieving such a goal.

The regeneration of Indian society, he believed, could take place only if the villages could be resuscitated. Villages were being exploited by the cities. They depended on the sufferance of cities. He wanted to build a healthy and moral relationship between the two. Although Gandhiji never thought hypothetically, he gave his conception of future India, "I shall work for an India in which the poorest shall feel that it is their country, in whose making they have an effective voice, an India in which there shall be no high class or low class of people, an India in which all communities shall live in perfect harmony..............There can be no room in such an India for the curse of untouchability or the curse of intoxicating drinks and drugs......Women will enjoy the same rights as men...... This is the India of my dream".

His Educational Philosophy

Before dealing with the educational philosophy of Gandhiji, it will be pertinent to know the background of his educational philosophy. There were several factors that determined his educational philosophy: (1) His educational experiments at Tolstoy Farm, Sabarmati and Sewagram Ashrams. These have been referred to under our first subhead; (2) His philosophy of life. Education being the dynamic side of philosophy, Gandhiji's philosophy of life determined his philosophy of education. He saw the realisation and means of his ideals of life in education; (3) His dissatisfaction with the prevailing system of education. System of education introduced by the English did not suit the country. English medium for all the branches of higher learning, in his view, was the greatest handicap. This had created a permanent bar between the highly educated few and the uneducated many. It had prevented knowledge from percolating to the masses. Teeming millions of India were wrought in ignorance, superstition, inertia and illiteracy. Whatever education was given to a small fraction of children was a waste as it was given in a passive manner. The child was a mere listener. Some smattering information was pumped into the child, without his realizing the value of the knowledge given to him. Education was not related to life. No training was given in power of observation. Practical work was conspicuous by its absence. No sense of citizenship was developed. Gandhiji was convinced that the prevailing system of primary education was not only wasteful but positively harmful. He remarked, "most of the boys are lost to the parents and to the occupation to which they are born. They pick up evil habits and affect urban ways". Such education was neither, "responsive to the realistic elements of the present situation, nor inspired by any life giving and creative ideal." (4) His conviction that social, moral, political and economic regeneration of India depended on education. He wanted to create a social order in which the conditions should be such that each man should be able to realise the highest aims of his life. He should not only adopt a policy of non-interference in others way of pursuing the same ideal, but he should actually help and co-operate with other fellow workers in their search after truth. Gandhiji believed that such a social order, based on Truth and non-violence, would exclude every type of exploitation, — economic, social, political or even religious.

Keeping in view the aforementioned factors Gandhiji evolved an absolutely new philosophy of education. By education he meant, "an all round drawing out of the best in child and man — body, mind and spirit". He said that literacy should never be the end of education nor even the beginning. "It is only one of the means whereby man and woman can be educated." True education, according to Gandhiji is that which draws out and stimulates the intellectual and physical faculties of the children. A sound education he believed, should produce useful citizens — whole men and whole women — of boys and girls. A whole man or woman is considered one, who has a harmonious development of all four aspects of the human personality — body, heart, mind and spirit. Any scheme of education, emphasising only one of these aspects of the personality is a lopsided education. This was the defect that he found in the prevailing system of education. No effort was being made to adjust the child intelligently and actively to his environment. Education, he took, "not in a parochial sense of a classroom process, but in its broad and true sense of a life long process which begins with the beginning and ends with the end of life going on constantly and unceasingly.

The chief tenets of his new educational philosophy were:

(1) that there should be free and compulsory primary education; (2) that the education should be craft centred; (3) that it should be self-supporting; (4) that it should be given in the mother tongue; (5) that it should be based on non-violence.

Free Compulsory Education: Mahatma Gandhi wanted, that within the ages 7 and 14 there should be free, compulsory universal primary education. His conception of primary education, was up to matriculation minus the English. In other words he wanted to combine the present primary and secondary education into one — called the English — less — Matriculation. For, he was convinced that children get nothing more in the high school than a half baked knowledge of English besides a superficial knowledge of mathematics and history and geography. If English is cut from the curriculum altogether, without cutting out the other subjects, the children in his opinion, can go through the whole course in 7 years instead of 10 or 11. Besides, the manual work can be added, whereby they can make a fair return to the state.

By this, he never meant that pre-primary or higher education should be neglected altogether. In his own words, "primary education, extending over a period of 7 years or longer, and covering all the subjects up to the Matriculation standard, except English, plus a vocation used as the vehicle for drawing out the minds of boys and girls in all departments of knowledge should take the place of what passes today under the name of primary, middle and high school education." He wanted that the state should also accept the responsibility of providing pre-school education as and when their finances permit them to do the same.

Regarding higher education, he said, "that it should be left to private enterprises and for meeting national requirements in the various industries, technical arts, belles letters or fine arts". He wanted that the State Universities should be there. But they should be purely examining bodies, supporting themselves through the fees charged for examination. Their function should also be to look after the whole field of education. They should prepare and approve courses of studies in the various departments of education. Of course every private school should be required to secure the previous sanction of their respective Universities. University charters should be given liberally to anybody or persons of proved worth and integrity. The University, however, should not cost the state anything. The state should have a Central Education Department. The state can also run such seminaries as may be required for supplying state needs.

Craft-Centred Education: Gandhiji believed that the highest development of mind and the soul was possible only through handicraft. He wanted to begin education of the child, "by teaching it a useful handicraft and enabling it to produce from the moment it begins its training. Thus every school can be made self-supporting, the condition being that the State takes over the manufactures of those schools". He did not want to teach the handicraft side by side with the liberal education. It was his wish that the "whole process of education should be imparted through some handicraft or industry". At the same time, he said, that the handicraft should not be taught mechanically but scientifically. That is, the child should know the why and wherefore of every process. For example, by teaching Takli-spinning knowledge of the various varieties of cotton, the different soils in different provinces of India, the history of the decay of handicraft, the political reasons for this, including the history of British rule in India, a knowledge of Arithmetic and so on should be imparted. The craft should not be taught, merely for production work but for developing the intellect of pupils. The manual training should not consist in producing articles for a school museum of toys, which have no value. It should produce marketable articles. The children should not do all this under compulsion or under whip, as was done in the early days of factories. They should do it because it interests them and stimulates their intellect.

Gandhiji never believed that the vocational bias will make education dull or cramp the child's mind. Children are sure to be bright and joyful if they receive vocational instruction under competent teachers. Just as Pestalozzi tried his methods on his own son, Mahatma Gandhi tried his methods on his grandson. He found that his grandson scarcely felt that he was being taught, because all the time he played and laughed and sang.

Besides wanting to do away with the machine, which had killed all sense of art and hand work, Gandhiji wanted such a craft which should have rich educative possibilities. "It should find natural points of correlation with important human activities and interests and should extend to the whole content of the school curriculum."

By teaching craft, his object was not to produce craftsmen but he wanted to exploit the craft for educative purposes. He wanted that, "stress should be laid on the principles of co-operative activity, planning, accuracy, initiative and individual responsibility in learning". He wanted that the craft should be learnt systematically and scientifically to serve as a means for intellectual work and economic self-sufficiency. The teaching of all subjects, Gandhiji said, should be inspired by the craft.

Self-Supporting Element: Gandhiji saw that as a nation Indians were so backward in education that they could not be educated if the programme was to depend on money. Crores of children could not wait until the Government found the necessary finances. He therefore, suggested that education should be self-supporting. It was his belief that handicraft, besides developing the personality of the child, would make education self-supporting.

His self-supporting aspect was criticised. The critics argued that when people should spend money on primary education Gandhiji was advocating the exploitation of children. They also feared that there would be enormous waste at the hands of small children. To this Gandhiji replied, "As for exploiting or burdening the children, I would ask whether we burden the child when we save him from disaster? The tukli is enough good toy to play with. It is no less a toy because it is a productive one. Even today children help their parents to a certain extent. The Segaon children know the details of agriculture better than I, for they have worked with their parents on the field. Whilst the child will be encouraged to spin and help his parents with agricultural jobs, he will also be made to feel that he belongs not only to his parents but also to the village and to the country, and that he must make some return to them... The children will become self-confident and 'brave if they pay for their own labour." He believed that, "without the use of hands and feet the brain would be atrophied, and even if it worked, it would be the home of Satan." There was yet another cause for making his education self-supporting. He said that free studentship, "lies and should be like a load upon a conscientious lad's mind throughout his life."

Some critics say that economic calculation in connection with education is sordid. But this is not so. India's circumstances demanded economic calculation. Money was scarce. Colossal illiteracy was to be broken. Mahatma Gandhi was conscious of it; Self-supporting education was the only alternative.

When he said that education through handicraft should be self-supporting, he meant that it should be self-supporting during the sum total of 7 years, the period which he prescribed for the primary education. He was conscious of the partial loss during the first years and wished that it should be made up in the following years. In this self-supporting aspect again he wanted the State to provide expenses for school buildings, furniture, books and all the apparatus and tools required for craft work.

By advocating the self-supporting aspect he never wanted the craft to be made the be-all and end-all of instruction, thus sacrificing the educative and cultural objectives of education. He believed that right kind of teachers would teach the children the dignity of labour and those children would regard the craft as an integral part and means of their intellectual growth.

Emphasis on Mother-tongue: Gandhiji emphasised mother-tongue both as a subject of study and as a medium of instruction. He found that the greatest handicap of the prevailing system of education was that learning was being imparted through the medium of English. This hindered the development of understanding and precision of thought or clarity of ideas. Mother-tongue, he believed, would enable the children not only to understand clearly the rich heritage of people's ideas; emotions and aspirations but would also enable the children to express themselves effectively, clearly and lucidly. They would, thereby appreciate and enjoy literature.

His Creed of Non-violence: A unique feature of Gandhiji's educational philosophy was the, "application of the law of non-violence in the training of the child as a prospective citizen of the world." Gandhiji was sick of communal and international strife and he wanted to create a generation which should believe in non-violence. This, he thought, to be the panacea for all evils. He said, "Where the whole atmosphere is redolent with the pure fragrance of ahimsa, boys and girls studying together will live like brothers and sisters in freedom and yet in self-imposed restraint; the students will be bound to the teachers in ties of filial love; mutual respect and mutual trust." Every act of students, he said, should be accomplished by love. His scheme of education wanted to bring an age from which "class and communal hatred is eliminated and exploitation is eschewed." Gandhiji emphatically remarked, "We cannot, will not think of exploitation, and we have no alternative but this plan of education which is based on non-violence."

Was he a Naturalist, an Idealist or a Pragmatist?

Although it may appear contradictory, Gandhiji synthesised all these three philosophies into his philosophy of education. He was a naturalist, idealist and pragmatist. When he advocates that children should be taught "in an atmosphere free from superimposed restriction and interference" he is a naturalist. But his 'freedom' is not a 'license', which may mean that the individual should be allowed to follow his own inclination, whims and caprices. Gandhiji emphasised 'discipline', regulated and well directed life. In this emphasis he was an idealist. He wanted to inculcate self-discipline among children and considered that time and money spent on education wasted if the children did not learn discipline in their school. Discipline, he believed, should not be imposed from without. There should be an inner urge of the individual to obey the laws and regulations prescribed by the group, community or society. It is in this conception of discipline that he synthesises naturalism and idealism. He wanted the children to have sufficient freedom so that they may develop and grow. But they must accept discipline and training if they want to develop their powers to the fullest. He believed in the inherent goodness of the child's nature and recognised that activity was the essential aspect of child's nature. He hated verbalism and wanted the child to lead a life of simplicity and naturalness rather than artificiality. On these grounds he may be declared as a naturalist.

Gandhiji was an idealist. As mentioned earlier he had a profound faith in God or the Universal Spirit, which permeates in everything. He, therefore, wanted man not only to aim at 'self-realisation' but also to realise God and be one with Him. Spiritual Realisation, in his view, should be the prime goal of life. Self-realisation, according to him, could be attained by self-abnegation and penance. Spiritual Realisation, he held, can be achieved by seeking after the Truth, practising Non-violence and doing Service to the Creatures of God. He considered spiritual realization as essential part of the training of the young. He said, "to develop the spirit is to build character and to enable one to work towards a knowledge of God and self-realisation...Training without culture of the spirit was of no use, and might be even harmful". His emphasis on harmonious development of personality included spiritual, intellectual, moral and physical development. These factors label him as an idealist.

From the above it appears that since Gandhiji believed in self-realisation and absolute truth — the creed of an idealist — he could not be pragmatist, but this is not true. He was a pragmatist in the same degree as an idealist and naturalist. He reconciled the practical and the spiritual values. It was through grappling with real situations of life that the child realised himself. Learning by experience was the chief motive behind his craft-centred education. Like Dewey he deems that as true which can be experimentally verified. Like him again, Gandhiji wanted his school to be a doing and a thinking school, instead of listening school. He wanted that all teaching should be carried on through concrete life situations relating to industry or to social and physical environment, so that whatever the child learns becomes assimilated into his growing activity. His was a school which was a place of work, experimentation and discovery instead of being a place of passive absorption of information imparted through books. His was an activity-curriculum like that of Dewey. Through activity the child acquires knowledge and utilizes it for the understanding and control of his social environment. This enabled the child to inculcate social responsibilities, which is the crying need of democratic India. His craft-centred education is an ample testimony that Gandhiji was a pragmatist. Relating education with real life situation, providing social experience to the child, emphasising learning by self-activity, minimising verbalism and bookishness, co-ordinating and correlating of the subjects of study are some of the features of Gandhian education which go to prove beyond any doubt that he was a pragmatist. Dr. M.S. Patel very aptly concludes Gandhiji's philosophy of education as, "naturalistic in his setting; idealistic in its aims and pragmatic in its method and programme of work".

Psychological Foundations of his Education

Mahatma Gandhi was a practical psychologist. The theory of education that he formulated after long thought and experience was not without psychological insight. Like Rousseau he restored the child to his rightful place and made education child-centric. He attached greater importance to the personality of the educand than to the tools and the subjects. For becoming a real teacher, he said the hearts of the children should be touched. Their joys and sorrows should be shared and they must be helped to solve their own problems. Their 'surging aspirations' must be directed to the right channel.

Conscious of child's natural instincts, Gandhiji made a full use of them by introducing the takli. The use of takli satisfied the child's instinct of play. But it was a play which was purposeful rather than frivolous. Similarly, the instincts of pugnacity and self- assertion were satisfied by competition of takli spinning among the children. 'Curiosity' was satisfied by knowing the why and wherefore of the cotton. Acquisitive instinct got its outlet when the children prepared some articles and considered them as their own.

Love and trust between the teacher and taught was the cardinal principle of Gandhiji's teachings. Through love, he said, the right type of teacher would be able to "draw forth the best that is in the child through understanding, sympathy, and appreciation of each child's precious individuality. Sweet compulsion of love should be the rule in education". This would "put the child on its own resources" and would also eliminate punishment. Once when two of the inmates of Tolstoy Farm showed moral fall, Gandhiji was shocked. He handled the situation wisely like a psychologist. Instead of resorting to "negative repression, reprimands, moralising and the 'don't method'" he brought about their change of heart by love, sympathy and understanding. In order to make them realise their fault, he observed a fast. This proved very efficacious in bringing the change.

He hated verbalism and the use of books. He wanted to depend upon the ears, eyes and hands. His emphasis, like Dewey, was on activities and occupations of real life. To him, the school was a projected home "with the same surroundings, same problems and same occupations". Handicrafts, according to him, would teach the child how to see, think and work when in grip with difficulties. This creates in the child self-reliance and self-confidence.

Gandhiji's plan of education was paedo-centric. His scheme based on activity and the study of the child, cannot be otherwise than child-centred. Activity and interest is the core of his scheme of education. But he wanted a purposeful activity like handicraft and manual work. His was a productive, remunerative and educative activity. His activity was a "prime means of intellectual training". It also strengthened the muscles of children and made them physically supple. Thus the activity co-ordinated the hand, the eyes and the ears. He remarked, "The hand will handle tools before it draws or traces the writing, the eyes will read the pictures of letters and words as they will know other things in life, the ears will catch the same and meanings of things and sentences." By putting into use the child's senses, he develops the power of observation and imagination.

Correlation with craft and with environment and co-ordination with subjects is another psychological factor which received the greatest attention of Gandhiji. He made the handicrafts the pivot, round which the teaching of other subjects like mathematics, history, geography, nature-study should revolve. He wanted an effective and natural correlation between the craft and other subjects and the co-ordination of various subjects.

His plan of education is psychological because it "relieves the child from the tyranny of purely academic and theoretical instruction against which its active instincts always make a healthy protest. It balances the intellectual and practical elements of experience and may be made an instrument of educating the body and the mind in co-ordination. The child acquires not the superficial literacy — a capacity to read the printed page — but the far more important capacity of using hand and intelligence for some constructive purpose." All these psychological foundations of his plan of education aimed at "literacy of the whole personality."

Gandhiji's Aims of Education

Being an idealist and a realist Gandhiji kept ultimate aim and immediate aims of education before him. Knowledge of God, self-realisation, spiritualism and oneness with God was the ultimate aim of education according to him. He laid great stress on 'the spirit' and declared that we should realise the spirit-force or soul-force instead of our being enthusiastic for 'evanescent, transitory and material force'. "True education should result not in the material power, but in spiritual-force". That explains his great stress on religious and moral education, which he thought, should teach the children fundamental virtues of truth, love, justice and non-violence. "Life without religion" Gandhiji held "is life without principle, and life without principle is like a ship without a rudder; and just as a ship without a rudder will be tossed about from peace to place and never reach a destination, so a man without religious backing be also tossed about on this stormy ocean of the world, without reaching the destined goal". God, according to him, could be achieved not by retiring into jungles, but by living in a society and serving it. He preferred to call a student 'brahmchari' a searcher after God. The means to achieve the knowledge of God and self-realisation are self-control, abstinence and character. Society, consisting of persons having such virtues will be a spiritual society, believing in non-exploitation, non-violence, truth, justice and equality for all. In such society religion would pervade in every action — political, economic, education or social.

In the immediate aims he included (1) the utilitarian aim; (2) the cultural aim; (3) harmonious development of one's personality; (4) preparation for complete living; (5) character building; (6) sociological aim or training for citizenship.

The Utilitarian Aim: Considering the basic needs of man's life as food, shelter and clothes, he advocated the self-supporting education. This self-supporting aspect was meant in two different senses, *viz*., (a) education that will help one to be self-supporting in later life; (b) education which meets its own way. According to the first sense Gandhiji wanted the child, at the age of 14, that is after finishing a seven years course to be an earning unit. This was in consonance with the circumstances, obtained in India. Poor peoples' children cannot afford to depend too much on their parents after this age. With this object he emphasised 'craft'. By this he did not want to turn the child into a base mechanic, but a self-respecting citizen, who would not be a drag on the society. By the second sense of 'self-supporting education' Gandhiji wanted that teachers' salaries should be met out of the productive work of the children, provided that the State takes over the manufacture of the school.

Cultural Aim : Cultural aim of education was not neglected by Gandhiji. Culture refines personality. Mere acquisition of knowledge is not enough for a man. He should have the quality of mind, which may be reflected in his daily conduct. Gandhiji attached greater importance to the cultural aspect of education than to the literary. He said "it should show itself in smallest details of your conduct and personal behaviour, how you sit, how you walk, how you dress etc. Inner culture must be reflected in your speech, the way in which you treat visitors and guests, and behave towards one another and your teachers and elders". According to him culture is not the product of intellectual work, but the quality of the soul, permeating all aspects of human behaviour. It is, therefore, an important function of education that children must be taught to have winsome conduct and the career.

Harmonious Development of One's Personality: As already mentioned Gandhiji meant by education, "an all round drawing out of the best in child and mind — body, mind and spirit". Harmonious development of all powers — innate and acquired was the chief goal of Gandhian education. "True education," he said, "must stimulate the spiritual, intellectual and physical faculties of the children". This all-round education, he believed could be given through craft. His emphasis was more on 3 H's (hand, heart and head) than on 3 R's (reading, writing and arithmetic). In order to draw the best out of the child and to create real interest in him, physical drill, handicrafts, drawing and music should go side by side. He was painfully conscious of the fact that prevailing system of education was unbalanced as it exercised only the training of the mind. Mental training, to him, appeared, nothing if it was "not accompanied by a true training of the heart. It is the harmoniously developed person that adjusts to his life and environments.

Preparation for Complete Living: Life is very complex in the present age. Gandhiji realised it and he formulated the scheme of education which would fit the child in later life. Coming into grip with problems and difficulties, he prepared the child to face the problems of life. A child was considered prepared for complete living if he could adjust himself to self, his occupation and his society.

Character Building: Nothing else appealed to Gandhiji more than the building of character as the chief aim of education. He made this the central purpose of education, and everything else was subordinated to this one purpose. By character Gandhiji did not mean merely a collection of certain skills, habits and principles of conduct. He regarded character as the expression of "the whole personality including its ethical and spiritual aspect". Again he did not conceive character as an unrelated phenomenon, "something self-contained and self-sufficient, independent, of its environment". He viewed it as a dynamic force proceeding towards a definite direction. An individual lives his own life, the life of the society or the nation he belongs to as well as the life of Universal Man. Therefore he must play his role in this drama of life well. He should conserve within himself the wisdom of the past, making full use of his national heritage. He should try to solve the problems which beset humanity. He must subordinate his own interests to the greater interest of society. Instead of working for personal gain he must co-operate and collaborate with his fellow beings for bringing about a new social order. If he can do this he is really a man of character.

Sociological Aim or Training for Citizenship: While he advocated self-supporting education, he aimed at producing useful citizens. This is the primary need of democratic India. The future citizens should understand their problems, rights and duties. They should know the co-operative institutions like Panchayats, Municipalities and District Boards which work for the good of all.

'Educate your masters' is the first slogan of democracy and Gandhiji advocated universal education. His aim was to create a classless society. Sociologically the introduction of craft in education "would break down the existing barriers of prejudices between manual and intellectual workers". Craft would produce the dignity of labour in the men. Instead of being parasites or drags on society every person would be an earning unit for the efficiency of the society. Everyone would play his role worthily. Education, therefore, should foster a keen sense of personal worth, desire for self-improvement and social service in co-operative community". Thus, he wanted to create a society based upon love, truth, justice, equality, brotherhood, co-operation and national solidarity. Sarvodaya Samaj was the cherished dream of Mahatma Gandhi. The aim of such Samaj should be the uplift of all, regardless of caste, creed and colour. Every member of this should have the spirit of courage, industry and self-sacrifice. Contented and happy humanity was the ideal of his plan of education.

Are These Aims Individual or Social?

An educational aim is social when the needs and the requirements of the society are uppermost. All that is taught and inculcated is conducive to the good of the society. Individual's aptitudes and inclinations are subordinated to this highest good. An educational aim is individual when education helps to make the life of individual better, richer and happier. The function of education, in that case, is to secure, "the conditions under which individuality" is most completely developed" and personality is exalted. Like Dewey, Gandhiji wants the synthesis of the two. He does not want to destroy the individuality, "which lies at the root of all progress — material and spiritual". This, he said, because he believed that no two persons are identical. They differ in nature, ability and temperament. But like Froebel, he wanted unity in diversity — the individual to develop "for the good of the whole without losing their individual character". He wanted the care of the individual and believed that the society will take care of itself. Here he resembles Rousseau in assigning the prime place to individual in a society. But unlike Rousseau he wants the individual to inculcate a spirit of service and sacrifice for the good of the society or state. He valued individual freedom but did not forget that man is essentially a social being. "Man", he said, "has risen to his present status by learning to adjust his individualism to the requirements of social progress.

Unrestricted individualism is the law of the beast of the jungle". He, therefore, wanted to "strike the mean between individual freedom and social restraint, as he believed that "willing submission to social restraint for the sake of the well being of the whole society, enriches both the individual and the society". To him individual development and social progress are not contradictory. They are complementary. He remarked, "if one man gains spiritually, the whole world gains with him...If one man falls, the whole world falls to that extent." Mahatma Gandhi echoes John Dewey when he says, "A nation cannot advance without the units of which it is composed advancing, and conversely, no individual can advance without the nation of which it is a part also advancing." Gandhiji held, "That the individual must work out his perfection in a spiritual society."

He did not agree with Rousseau that the individual can develop in a social vacuum. Self-realisation and social service must go hand in hand. Individual, according to him, "can make the best of himself in a state and the state can achieve its highest development only on the condition that each of its citizen gives the best that is in him." The individual develops in a social atmosphere. It is there that it can have common 'interest and can engage himself in common activities. Like John Dewey, Gandhiji wanted to transform the schools into communities where individuals get abundant opportunities of social contact and co-operation.

Gandhiji synthesised the individual and the social aims of education. He proved it by example and precept that 'self-relisation' and 'social service' were not contradictory. A fusion of the two in a man made the man complete.

His Curriculum

In order to acquire "the essential modicum of social and civic training" Gandhiji wanted a syllabus which should enable the child to adjust himself intelligently and actively to his physical and social environment and to craft work "which is their natural meeting point since it utilises the resources of the former (physical) for the purposes of the latter (social)". His attempt, therefore, was to plan an activity curriculum which should transform the schools into "places of work, experimentation and discovery". In his curriculum he included the following subjects:

(1) Basic craft which may be agriculture or spinning and weaving or card board; wood and metal work. (2) Mother tongue. (3) Mathematics. In this more emphasis is to be laid on numerical and geometrical problems connected with craft and community life. He wished that children should learn four simple rules by actually working out the problems arising out of craft work and gardening. They should deal with figures which may throw light on the economic and social facts of their village, town or country. This practical measuring and field work and calculations of expenditure and of rural indebtedness would make the learning of mathematics an active process. This would enable the learner to interpret and understand the social environments. An acquaintance with business practice and book-keeping is also essential. (4) Social studies, which should include history, geography and civics. (5) General science in which should be included nature study, Zoology, Physiology, Hygiene, Physical culture, Chemistry and knowledge of stars. (6) Drawing and Music was included to create in boys and girls a real interest in education. Primary education, he said, must include the elementary principles of sanitation, hygiene, nutrition, doing their own work, helping parents at home etc. Realising the physical difficulties of the present generation he prescribed compulsory physical training through musical drill.

Up to the fifth grade of the school the curriculum was to be the same for both girls and boys. In the later stages general science and craft were to be replaced by domestic science in case of girls.

His Estimate

In Gandhiji we find a combination of man of thought and man of action. With him to know was to act. Whatever Gandhiji said and propounded had the backing of experience. He formulated his ideas, tested them and where necessary corrected them in the light of his experience. Whole of his life was devoted to translating his thoughts into actions. That is why he entitled his autobiography as 'Experiments with Truth'. If he prescribed handicraft he had himself taught sandal making and spinning with good results.

He dedicated his life to the pursuit of Truth and Non-violence. All the human elements in his personality came into play and showed how loving and lovable he was and what immense capacity he had to bind men to himself "by the golden links of reverence, affection and confidence". He has shown us that the ultimate object of man's life is self-realisation, seeing God face to face and realising the Absolute Truth. For this realisation he indicated the means as non-violence.

The main objectives of his educational plan may be summed up in his own words, "my plan to impart primary education through the medium of village handicrafts....is thus conceived as the spearhead of a silent social revolution — fraught with the most far reaching consequences. It will provide a healthy and moral basis of relationship between the city and the village and thus go a long way towards eradicating some of the worst evils of the present social insecurity and poisoned relationship between the classes. It will check the progressive decay of our villages, and lay the foundation of a juster social order in which there is no unnatural division between the haves and have-nots and everybody is assured of a living wage and the right to freedom. And all this would be accomplished without the horrors of a bloody class war or a colossal capital expenditure such as would be involved in the mechanisation of India. It would place the destiny of the masses in their own hands." Mahatma Gandhi revolutionised the whole concept of education. Basic scheme is the most practical and unique contribution of Gandhiji. In the words of B.G. Kher it would produce, "socially more alert and intelligent and more co-operative" citizens having "a keener consciousness of their relationship to the community." He was the first educationist to advocate the large scale use of handicraft, not only as a productive work but as a pivot round which the teaching of all subjects should be undertaken. He put forward a system which is inexpensive and also in consonance with the needs of our vast rural population. In no other way could primary education be made free, compulsory and effective.

A new social order — known as the Sarvodaya Samaj was his great dream. Such society would be classless. Individual will be conscious of spiritual reality. They will lead a life of simplicity, service and sacrifice. There would be no exploitation but equality and justice. The chief means of achieving this new social order, according to Gandhiji, is education. Education centred round handicraft would produce generation which instead of being drones on the society would be its useful and earning members.

Mahatma Gandhi's thoughts are in line with the best educational thought both in the East and in the West. His objective of education — both immediate and ultimate — are suited to the genius of Indian culture and heritage. Basic education has now come out of experimental age and is being tried on a very large scale. Given the proper type of missionary teachers, its success is a guarantee. Earnest effort on the part of the Government and the co-operative spirit on the part of the public will go a long way in making the scheme efficacious. For its successful working Gandhiji made a clarion call to the educationists who have no axes to grind. He never wanted persons who wrangle at loaves and fishes. If the educationists work out the scheme without preconceived notions, there is no reason why the colossal problem of educating the masses should not be solved. "Only they must have a living faith in it. Such faith can only grow from within, it cannot be acquired vicariously."

Like all other educators discussed before, recognition and appreciation of his theories and experiments came to him during his life time. Although recognised and accepted in India, Gandhiji's philosophy of education has not yet accepted universal recognition. But that time is not far off, when his philosophy will be accepted by all nations as the only way to world peace and progress. There is reason to believe that educational practice all over the world may be influenced by his teachings. His dream of world full of love, fellow-feeling and free from greed and exploitation can be realised if his philosophy is followed. He proved it by his example and precept that inherently human heart is good. Only conditions and opportunities have to be created to develop that goodness. This is the only way to have one world "knit together by bonds of affection and brotherhood".

A great guide, teacher and benefactor of mankind was born in India and sacrificed his life and all for regeneration — political, social, educational and economic — of India. In the words of Dr. Rajendra Prasad, "Indians, remembering the great service, supreme sacrifice and ultimate martyrdom of Mahatma Gandhi must rely upon truth, service and love as the inexhaustible sustenance of life. They must march on towards the glorious goal of establishment of social justice and human equality in (India) and in maintenance of the peace in the world. His soul would rest in peace when the teaming millions of rural India understand the benefits of democracy. It is only possible through education which must get the highest priority among the nation-building activities."

Some Criticism of his Scheme

There is a section of educators who believe that there "is more of sentiment than of sound educational philosophy" behind Gandhiji's ideas. They argue that since the scheme is connected with the name of the Father of the Nation and a Great Saviour of India, therefore, it is being advocated and followed. Even if it is true it is not a bad thing to have a sentiment for a good scheme. This sentiment is not based upon any extraneous factor but on inherent merits of the scheme. No one can deny that India had to be regenerated socially, morally, intellectually and politically through education. For this the cheapest method and a method suiting to the genius of our traditions and circumstances had to be found. Colossal illiteracy, ignorance and squalor had to be broken. Means to fulfil the requirements of rural India had to be explored. Mahatma Gandhi found these means, and then, his educational ideas in no way violate the psychological and pedagogical principles.

A group of educationists feel that all subjects cannot be correlated with craft, as they believe, to have been said by Gandhiji. But did Gandhiji have such a narrow conception of correlation? By suggesting the maximum use of correlation he wanted to give greater concreteness and reality to the knowledge acquired by children. Correlation for him had a wider connotation. Besides correlating the teaching of subjects with craft, he desired to utilize other processes in teaching. The object was that education should be related to life environments — physical, social and economic.

Some critics believe that introducing craft-centred education is putting the clock back. They argue that spinning and weaving era, as a matter of fact, any craft looks out of tune in the modern machine age. But they forget that basic education was advocated chiefly for rural areas, where more than 75 per cent of the population of India lives. That is why he calls his scheme of education as Rural National Education. The crafts selected are in consonance with the village situation. Such crafts would tend to make the education more concrete and real than any reference to modern amenities, which would take years to enter the precincts of the villages. Again it must be understood that the craft is the means and not an end itself.

It will not be out of place to conclude that there is nothing final and perfect. It is the experience, experimentation and modification in the light of experience that takes us nearer and nearer perfection.

Comparison with Others

Like Rousseau, Gandhiji restored the child to his legitimate place in the scheme of education. His education was child-centred. Both of them were against verbalism and wanted the child to work with his own hand for the development of his mind. As referred earlier, Rousseau believed in negative education. He wanted the child to learn by error, but Gandhiji's approach was positive and he wanted to make efforts that the child should not commit any error.

Coming to Pestalozzi we can say that if Pestalozzi was called 'Father Pestalozzi' Gandhiji was called the 'Father of Nation'. Both of them stood for the harmonious development of human personality. Pestalozzi advocated education for all. So was the ideal of Gandhiji. Both of them had agriculture and spinning and weaving as the main crafts which must be taught to the child. However, Pestalozzi did not lay much emphasis upon the correlation of craft with the teaching of other subjects, while with Gandhiji this was the main emphasis.

Froebel and Gandhiji agree at many points. The former said that the innate propensities of the child must not be allowed to lie dormant. They must be aroused. Gandhiji also said that function of education is to arouse the natural powers to their fullest development. Both of them saw spiritual meanings behind every activity. With both self-activity was the chief principle of learning. The importance of social environment was recognised by both. Gandhiji and Froebel are in complete accord as far as the divine unity or God is concerned. Both of them believed that God pervades in everything and that the knowledge about him is the ultimate aim of education.

The two great 'activists' — Mahatma Gandhi and John Dewey — have many common features of educational philosophy. Both of them are realists and pragmatists. They believe in doing and not listening and talking in education. Their ideal of relating the school with society are identical. Their children learn in Co-operative Community and Social experience. Intellectual education is advocated by them through crafts and occupations and both of them agree that education should be self-supporting. 'Construction, expression and activity' are the cardinal principles of their teaching methods. Both of them stood for the democratic order of society, the sustenance of which should be love, equality and justice.

Comparing Tagore with Gandhiji we can see that both of them make their educational system the vehicle of their philosophy of life. Gandhiji's truth and non-violence are akin to Tagore's message of love and universal brotherhood. Towards life, however, they have distinct attitudes. Gandhiji evolves a philosophy of action, or a Karma Yog philosophy, suited to the needs and abilities of each and every man. Tagore centred his philosophy on the eternal Anand, although he does not exclude action. Gandhiji's emphasis was on abiding values of life and on social purpose. Tagore's emphasis was on abiding values only.

Both of them make life as the centre of education. They want a curriculum which should provide opportunities for the expression of individual and community life. In their view a school should have the environment and programme in such a manner as to capture the spirit of Life. Both Tagore's ideal of education and basic education give a very prominent place to hand work or craft. While the former emphasises the creative and artistic aspect of hand work, the latter emphasises the social and economic aspect besides the creative. The basic scheme envisages that properly organised craft-centred education would break social barriers, teach the dignity of labour, increase the productive capacity and would give concreteness and reality to the knowledge. Tagore gives this concreteness to knowledge in expressional forms like art, music and dramatics. Principle of activity, however, is recognised by both of them; although basic education has gone into greater details in actual practice. The emphasis of both is the child-centric education. Education should be joyous to the child. The important role that Nature plays in the Education of the child is more obvious in Tagore's system, while such a thing is only implied in basic education.

In conclusion it can be said that the 'activity principle' in education was advocated by all great thinkers and educators from Comenius to Gandhiji.

8

Aurobindo Ghosh

(AUGUST 15,1872 — AUGUST 15,1947)

In the galaxy of saints, seers, sages and prophets in India, Aurobindo outshines all because of his versatile genius sprawling over the whole human situation — man individual, man collective, man temporal and man spiritual. The gigantic sweep of his philosophy of life centered round the transforming power of man, whom he wanted to develop the "soul-force" through the realisation of *Sublime Truth*. On this infrastructure he built his most well-articulated philosophy of education, the genesis of which is rooted in his kaleidoscopic career and his crystallised philosophy of life.

Born with a Divine Spark

It may be an unusual phenomena and extraordinary fortuity, but it is a reality that Sri Aurobindo's life gives lie to the psychological belief that environment makes the texture of one's thinking and personality. The eloquent testimony to this is borne by the fact that natured and nurtured in Western education and influence for 21 years, Aurobindo remained unscathed by the alien influences and the fire of Indian philosophy remained dormant in him to be manifested at an opportune moment.

Coming events cast their shadows before. Great men have a kaleidoscopic career. It is really so in case of Aurobindo, whose destiny went on shaping its own ends. Born to Krishnadhan (father) and Swaranlata (mother) on the 15th August, 1872 Aurobindo justified his progeny by his divine life in the acquisition of Krishnadhana (spiritual wealth of Lord Krishna) and blossomed as a flower of the golden creeper (Swaranlata). Being enamoured of Western culture, Dr. Krishnadhan sent Aurobindo at the age of 5 to Loretto Convent School at Darjeeling. Two years later he took him to England and put him in an English family, the Drewetts of Manchester, where Aurobindo joined the Grammar School. Mr. Drewetts taught him Latin at home. In 1885 Aurobindo went to St. Paul's school in London, whose Headmaster gave him good grounding in Greek. Five years' stay in this school gave him great proficiency in the classics. Thence he went to King's College, Cambridge where his scholarship had full bloom in terms of being the winner of all the prizes. For his mastery of French, German, Italian and Sanskrit and several other Indian languages, he had no peer as a linguist.

Aurobindo appeared at the Indian Civil Service examination in 1890 and passed it with credit, obtaining record marks in Greek and Latin. Perhaps not cut out for the I.C.S. he missed the riding test at the end of his probationary period to dedicate his life not to the mundane life of an I.C.S. (Indian Civil Service) but to I.S.S. (Indian Soul Service). Since remittances from his father became irregular and inadequate, he faced financial straits. Incidentally he happened to meet in England the Gaekwar of Baroda, who offered him a job in his State. Aurobindo left for India in 1893. Before he touched the Indian shore, his father died of the shock on receiving an incorrect news that the steamer by which Aurobindo had sailed was wrecked at sea near Lisbon and that Aurobindo did not survive.

From 1893 to 1905 he lived in Baroda at various jobs, the last being the Vice-Principal of a College, in addition to being the private secretary to the Maharaja. During this period, he got married and also became imbued with India's spirituality. In 1904 destiny took another turn. Aurobindo attended the Indian National Congress Session. Bengal was partitioned in 1905. This angered Aurobindo who wrote to his wife, "I find a demon is sitting astride of the breast of the mother and sucking her life-blood. It is my earnest endeavour to save the Mother from the clutches of the demon, not by brute force but by soul force". The call of the motherland compelled him to leave Baroda. He came to Calcutta and threw himself into the nationalist movement, which gathered momentum day-by-day.

Since the nation faced the grave problem of providing educational facilities to the students who had boycotted schools and colleges, a National College was established and Aurobindo was appointed Principal on Rs. 150 a month. This assignment gave him the opportunity to develop his own conception of national education. It is a matter of history that this college became the nucleus of the present Jadavpur University of technology-*cum*-humanities. Along with his Principalship, he was engaged in political activities through his writings, speeches and inspiration to his fellow country men.

The wheel of destiny took another round. In 1907 Aurobindo went to Baroda. One reputed Yogi Vishnu Bhaskar Lele, influenced him for Yoga. In the meantime national movement took a very serious turn and Aurobindo was arrested in 1908. By irony of circumstances he was tried by Mr. C. P. Beachcraft, the Sessions Judge, who was once his I.C.S. mate Aurobindo excelling Beachcraft in Greek. Mr. Craft seeing Aurobindo in the dock, remarked: "He is the accused whom more than any other the prosecution was anxious to have convicted and but for his presence in the dock, there is no doubt the case would have finished long ago". In his thrilling oration. Mr. C. R. Dass, the defence council of Aurobindo brilliantly said, "If you credit him with intellectual powers and say that he has a brilliant mind, it is not open to you at the same time to say that he was the leader of a childish conspiracy and a toy revolution. My appeal to you, therefore, is that a man like this who is being charged with the offences imputed to him stands not only before the bar in this court but stands before the bar of the High Court of History and my appeal is this: That long after this controversy is hushed in silence, long after this turmoil, this agitation ceases, long after he is dead and gone, he will be looked upon as the poet of patriotism, as the prophet of nationalism and lover of humanity. Long after he is dead and gone his words will be echoed and re-echoed, not only in India, but across distant lands and seas." (How prophetic were the words of Mr. C. R. Dass!) Aurobindo was discharged.

It was in the jail that spiritual light came upon him. He was blessed with a divine vision, the vision of Vasudeva, God, the supreme being. On his release he felt a call for a far deeper life, retired to Pondicherry on April 4, 1910 and devoted himself to expound his spiritual philosophy of Sublime Truth. Being a man with vast erudition and dynamic thinking, his vision and profundity resulted in delineating transcendental ideas on life, existence, society, state and world peace. Crowning all these was his epistemologies of Mind, superman, yoga and education.

The Great Philosophy

The summum bonum of the great philosophy of Sri Aurobindo can be summed up in one phrase "Realisation of the Sublime Truth", which can be achieved through the "Integral view of life", "Being a Superman and the Gnostic Individual", "Descent of Divine Power", "Intuition", "Yoga" and "Super-mind", and unflinching faith in the Trinity (spirituality, creativity and intellectuality) of Indian genius.

By integral view of life, he implied "a healthy integration of God and Man. According to him, the fellowship between God and Man generates in 'Man' an idea of new birth and new ideal of work and this fellowship can be achieved by man's disinterested action in society, by never ending meditation, by self-forgetting devotion and by feeling a kind of unity of all things in God.

Complete surrender of man to God, according to Aurobindo creates a superman, who transcends his own nature by rising above the qualities of Sattva, Rajas and Tamas. Such a man attains union with God in body, mind and soul and becomes a Jnani (ज्ञानी) or a Gnostic individual, who in the words of Aurobindo is "the consummation of spiritual man; his whole way of being, thinking, living and acting is governed by the power of a vast universal spirituality. He feels the presence of the Divine in every centre of his consciousness. All beings are to him his own-selves. The gnostic individual is in the world and out of the world, but also exceeds it in his consciousness and lives in his life of transcendence above it."

When man attains union with God in body, mind and soul, the Divine power descends on him and this helps him to fulfil his cosmic purpose and divine energy radiates from him into the world.

For arriving at the great spiritual tracks, Aurobindo placed premium on "Intuition" and not purely on logical reasoning and preached the gospel of "Intuition and more perfect intuition".

The integral view of life culminates in synthetic Yoga, which Aurobindo defines as "A methodised effort towards self-perfection by the expression of the potentialities latent in the being". In order to find a true basis of harmony and peace, man must rise to a consciousness higher than the limited and ignorant mind and reason. It is in the silent mind that the higher consciousness can be built. Yoga for getting settled peace and silence in the mind, Aurobindo staunchly advocates the practice of Yoga. Unlike others, his concept of Yoga does not "mean weaning away from life into seclusion and asceticism". He saw the imperfections of the life of man, but his Yoga did not run away from life in search of perfection. He considered Yoga as the remedy to eliminate the ills and imperfections of life and help human life to be turned into something divine. He said, "The very first lesson in this Yoga is to face life and its trials with a quiet mind, a firm courage and an entire reliance on the Divine Shakti". His Yoga was "free from the difficult feats of physical postures (Asana and Pranayama) and mechanical exercise in concentration". He recommended "an absolute and unconditional surrender to God as the first step of Yoga". His Yoga aimed at divinising the whole man and for this he advised thc education of the mind.

Theory of Mind

Sir William Hamilton once said, "In the world there is nothing great but man: in man there is nothing great but mind?". In exalting the realm of mind, no other philosopher, either in the West or in the East, comes nearer to Sri Aurobindo in breadth and comprehensiveness. He envisages a world in which life and mind work harmoniously and achieve the truth by transformation and transmutation of them in the light of the highest. According to him, the main instrument of thought is mind, which has immense and diverse powers. He considered mind as having four layers, which he identified as 'chitta', the 'Manas', 'intellect and intuition'. The first layer or 'chitta' is that of passive memory. It is a store-house of memories or past impressions. From this the active memory picks up the needed things when interest or action in life so warrants. The images of the passive memory do not remain in the forefront of consciousness. This region of passive memory is automatic and organically sufficient for its purposes and requires no training. The active memory, however, needs training and improvement. Sri Aurobindo says that while passive memory retains the past impressions without its being aware of it, the active memory remains aware of the past impressions. These ideas of his are comparable to modem researches about the unconscious and the sub-conscious.

The second layer of the mind is called the 'Manas' (or the mind proper). This receives the images coming from the five senses (touch, smell, taste, sight and sound) and transforms those images into thought perceptions. The mind, in addition to images received from the senses is also capable of having direct grasping of image or mental impressions. Aurobindo, therefore, calls 'mind' as the sixth sense. What we call telepathy, clairvoyance, and clairaudience in the modern times Aurobindo attributes them to be the powers of the mind through the pure action of the *Manas*. The yogic discipline aims at the development of the *Manas* in its pure actions and facilitates the reception of the images of far-off things and apprehends the phenomena much too subtle for the senses to perceive. Training of the sixth sense or the *Manas* is included in the educational ideology of Aurobindo. He has strongly pleaded for the introduction of elementary yogic practices into our schools and colleges.

The intellect of 'Budhi' is the third layer, where the elements of the knowledge are arranged and re-arranged. The intellect has comprehensive, creative, synthetic and analytical faculties. Sri Aurobindo regards creative faculties of the intellect as the right hand of 'Budhi' and analytical faculty as Budhi's left hand. The right hand imagines, judges, and manipulates, while the left hand compares, classifies and concludes. These faculties are the essentials of logical reasoning. The right hand is the master of knowledge as it penetrates deeply. The left hand mind is only a servant as it only touches the body of the knowledge. Both these hands of mind must be perfectly trained.

In view of the existence of geniuses in the world Aurobindo maintained that there is a phase of mind far higher than the intellect or *Budhi*. This fourth layer of the mind, he calls intuition, which "brings to man those brilliant messages from the unknown, which are the beginning of his higher knowledge". There are people who are far superior to others by reason of their direct immediate perception of truth, their sovereign power of discernment, inspiration and vision. The extraordinary powers of geniuses show that there is an intuitive fringe of every act of intellection, which is not developed in common man. Pure intuition, however, is a rare occurrence. He said, "if intuition had not been there, humanity would not have reached the present progressive stage". He, therefore, enjoins upon the teacher not to stifle by routine-work the genius in the pupils and rightly deplores that our present system of education does not have provision for the identification of the genius, his nurture and growth. The superiority-feeling of the teacher stands in the way of marking out geniuses, who are to all intents and purposes, much ahead of their fellow-students, sometimes even their teachers. The teacher, therefore, should be a psychologist so as to be able to follow with precision the subtle working of the human mind and to be liberal in his outlook.

Supermind

Aurobindo's theory of mind culminates in his belief of the existence of supermind. He explains that 'Mind' is being steadily pushed by evolutionary nisus. The frontiers of the mind go on extending through *Knowledge*, which passes through three stages; sense-knowledge is the characteristic of the normal mind; creative knowledge is the characteristic feature of the refined mind and self-effectuating, dynamic and illumined knowledge is the feature of a still higher principle in the scale of evolution of mind. "The higher plane of consciousness" is called the *supermind*. Aurobindo wanted that "the errors of the conceptual mind must be corrected by the supermind". "Supermind is the divine gnosis which creates, governs and upholds the world. It is a self-force of God. It is omnipotent, omniscient and omnipresent. This state of higher consciousness, one can acquire gradually. After acquiring it one must use it for transforming the entire being." Acquisition of such a mind is the chief task of Education.

The Trinity of the Indian Genius

The *tour de force* to his philosophic soarings was supplied by the Trinity of the Indian Genius. Finding his countrymen in a state of want, inferiority complex, unhappiness and tension he awakened them to the new age that was dawning upon them by reminding them of the Trinity of their Genius: spirituality, creativity, intellectuality.

Talking about the eternal *spirituality* of India, he said, "Spirituality is indeed the master key of the Indian mind, the sense of the infinite is native to it. The note of spirituality is dominant, initial, constant, always recurrent; it is the support of all the rest.

The first age of India's greatness was a spiritual age when she sought passionately for the truth of existence through the intuitive mind and through an inner experience and interpretation both of the psychic and physical existence. The stamp put on her by that beginning she has never lost, but rather always enriched it with fresh spiritual experience." He wanted this spirituality to be enriched rather than depleted. It was to the enrichment of this spirituality that Aurobindo devoted his life.

This spirituality, he correctly averred, did not flourish in the void but blossomed and flowered in the prolific *creativeness* of India. He said, "For three thousand years at least...... India has been creating abundantly and incessantly lavishly, with an inexhaustible many sidedness, republics and kingdoms and empires, philosophies and cosmogonies and sciences, creeds, arts, and poems...systems of Yoga, arts spiritual, arts worldly...the list is endless and in each item there is almost a plethora of activity".

To him Indian intellectuality, the third characteristic of Indian genius, is "at once austere and rich, robust and minute powerful and delicate, massive in principle and curious in detail". Sri Aurobindo exalted the Indian Culture as harmonious blend of "an ingrained and dominant spirituality, an inexhaustible vital creativeness and gusto of life, and mediating between them, a powerful, penetrating and scrupulous intelligence, combined of the rational, ethical, and aesthetic mind at a high intensity of action".

He asks: "What was the secret of that gigantic intellectuality, spirituality and superhuman moral force which we see pulsating in the epics, in the ancient philosophy, in the supreme poetry, art, sculpture and architecture of India? What was at the basis of the incomparable public works and engineering achievement, opulent and exquisite industries, the great triumphs of science, scholarship, jurisprudence, logic, metaphysics, the unique social structure? What supported the heroism and self-abandonment of the Kshatriya, the Sikh and the Rajput, the unconquerable national vitality and endurance. What was it that stood behind that civilization second to none in the massiveness of its outlines or the perfection of its details"?

He deplored the deterioration and decadence of these key-traits of Indian genius in the process of time and inspired the

Indian Renaissance in the words: "The recovery of the old spiritual knowledge and experience in all its splendour, depth and fullness is its first most essential work; the flowing of this spirituality into new forms of philosophy, literature, art, science and critical knowledge is the second, and original dealing with modern problems in the light of Indian spirit and the endeavour to formulate a greater synthesis of spiritualised society is the third and most difficult". He concludes the rhetoric by saying, "Without a great and unique discipline involving a perfect education of soul and mind, a result so immense would have been impossible". It is in education that Aurobindo finds the consummation of his philosophy.

Education as Consummation of Philosophy

Education being the dynamic side of philosophy, every philosopher is ultimately an educator. Philosophy determines the fundamental postulates of life — its meaning and aims. Education becomes the instrument of realising those aims. The superstructure of Aurobindo's educational philosophy was, therefore, built on the fundamentals of his philosophy as expounded above. His philosophy of education instead of being conceived in vacuum, was empiric and the result of perspective analysis and profound thought. The master-mind made a thorough work of his educational philosophy not only by spelling out his concept and aims of education, but suggested the curriculum design and the fundamentals of instructional technique in conformity with the aims and the new role of the teacher in helping the learner to achieve self-fulfilment.

Perspective Analysis

Aurobindo was thoroughly disgusted with the prevailing system of education which ignored the psychology of the learner, whose mind "was laboriously loaded with numerous little packets of information carefully tied with red-tape". "Information", he said, "cannot be the foundation of intelligence. It can only be a part of the material out of which the student builds the knowledge. It is only a starting point, a nucleus of fresh discovery and further creativity. An education that confines itself to imparting information is no education". To him the prevailing system required "the student to absorb without strengthening the body and the brain sufficiently to grapple with the increased mass of intellectual toil. This system followed the methods which damaged or atrophied the faculties and instruments by which man assimilates, creates and grows in intellect, manhood and energy".

He was pained to see the deterioration and decadence of the key-traits of Indian genius (spirituality, creativity and intellectuality), as a result of which, "Creation is replaced by lifeless imitation, intelligent appreciation is replaced by despotic authority of rules, balanced spiritual synthesis is replaced by overemphasis on certain spiritual truths. Diseased spirituality is the cause of decadence". He, therefore, wanted a different type of education.

His Concept

Aurobindo wanted a system of education "which sought immensely to enlarge the field of knowledge of the student and activised his memory, judgement and creative power; which laid stress on experiment and observation and encouraged the play of thought on the subject of study; which corrected the habit of spoiling the instruments of knowledge and employed, the natural and easy instrument of mother tongue". The advocacy of mother- tongue as the medium of instruction being made by one, who had his entire education through English medium shows his conviction of the merit of mother-tongue to be the natural medium of instruction. He was of the opinion that children should be introduced to foreign language "only when they can read and write in the mother tongue fairly well and have developed the mental instrument to such an extent as to be able to analyse the structure of sentences and propositions and appreciate pretty phrases and graceful idioms. In this way, they can make a great economy of time and energy and can have the command of language in question at a comparatively short time". His vital concern was that the children should learn their mother tongue properly before they proceed to learn any language.

Being a nationalist to the core he wanted that education must be all 'national', meaning thereby that it must be based upon the traditions of the nation. Nevertheless he warned that "mere inclusion of the matter of Indian thought and culture in the field of knowledge does not make a system of education Indian". He wanted "the spirit, ideals and methods of ancient and mightier India in a more effective form and with a more modern organisation". He inspired 'renaissance' in India and wanted this re-awakening and rebirth to take three directions:

1. The recovery of old spiritual knowledge and experience in all its spendour, depth and fulness:
2. The flowing of this spirituality into new form of philosophy, literature, arts, science and critical knowledge. In other words he wanted that India should keep her *essential spirit* and *her characteristic soul* but bring a change in the body, that is the new body for new philosophical, artistic, literary, cultural, political and social forms as in conformity with the emergent needs, demands and aspirations of resurgent and awakening India.
3. The original dealings with modern problems in the light of Indian spirit and the endeavour to formulate a greater synthesis of spiritualised society.

It is in this way, he thought, can be rejuvenated.

His Aims of Education

"The chief aim of education", according to Aurobindo "should be to help the growing soul to draw out that in itself which is best and make it perfect for a noble use." Mahatma Gandhi also defined education as "drawing out the best in man in body, mind and spirit". To Aurobindo, the real meaning of life is to rise above "ego" and to possess the "self". True education helps man to this goal. Education should help man to realise that he is vital, a mental, a psychic, supra-mental and supreme spiritual being. It should help him to develop his intellectual and moral capacities to their highest limit.

Aurobindo said that man is a soul inwardly and a conscious power of the divine. The evocation of this conscious power of the divine is the real aim of education. The fulfilment of individual does not consist in the growth of his egoistic intellect and maximum satisfaction of his physical, emotional and mental cravings but the developing of the divine in him to the maximum limit of power, love, wisdom and universality. Through this development he will attain the maximum realisation of all the possible beauty and delight of existence. Education should cater to this development.

He considered that education as "true and living which helps one to develop his latent powers and enables him to enter into the right relations with life, mind and soul of his nation as well as with the total life, mind and soul of humanity". "Man", he says, "has developed certain vital propensities and ego, a mind and a reason." His education should be so guided as to satisfy these propensities under the control of trained mind and reason.

Education of the Mind

Evolving a sophisticated theory of mind (as stated earlier), Aurobindo considered mind as the sixth sense and asserted that "the first business of the educationist is to develop in the child the right use of the six senses; to see that they are not stunted or injured by disuse, but trained by the child himself under the teacher's direction to that perfect accuracy and keen subtleness of which they are capable". "Mind must be perfectly trained to the highest possible limit, otherwise the education of the child will remain incomplete and one-sided." He wanted to reform our mind first before reforming the world. Education cannot be a machine-made fabric. It should aim at building the powers of the mind. According to him, "The utilization of the super-mind for the development of an integrated human personality" is the true aim of education.

He recognised three minds: the individual mind, the mind of a nation and the universal mind and pleaded for their consideration in education. Viewing "the building of the power of mind and spirit" as the central aim of education, he wanted the teacher to understand "the human mind at all the stages of development, infancy, childhood, adolescence and adulthood".

Aurobindo recognises two qualities of mind.

1. **Well disciplined or well structured mind:** It is well equipped with basic tools of thought and communication, and trained powerfully and precisely to (a) observe accurately and discriminatively (b) to think clearly (c) to criticise judiciously and (d) to remain well-informed.

2. **Individualised or well-textured mind:** It has a factor of uniqueness and originality and achieves the richest and fullest self-realisation. It is a lively mind, mind in ferment-insatiably curious, critical, imaginative and creative. A person whose mind has these two qualities for mind is a 'complete man', 'whole man', and 'integrated man', who rises above 'ego' and instead of following impulsive cravings, develops love, wisdom and universality and grows through spirituality, creativity and intellectuality.

Sri Aurobindo deplored the absence of "education of the mind" and appealed that this should be vital part of our education so as to make the mind creative, observant and discriminative. According to him mind functions through environmental stimulus as well as is "self-active". Education of the mind unfolds personality and helps in establishing right relationships. It is through the medium of education that he wants to develop mind to super-mind.

His Curriculum Design

Disgusted with the prevailing curricular trends, Aurobindo protested against the loading of the curriculum by asking the learner to learn something of everything. Instead of shallowness and superficiality in many subjects, he wants intensive knowledge in a few subjects.

Being a votary of ancient Indian culture and civilization, which contained profound wisdom and skill to transform the society and the individual towards the realisation of the infinite and create a discipline for spiritual perfection, Aurobindo wanted the study of Indian History and Culture to be an essential ingredient of the curriculum. He assumes that every child has a sense of history. Though this sense is not quite conscious and articulate in the beginning, it expresses itself in the form of 'fancy' and love of fables among the children. An analysis of children's play and their play-things reveal the ideal world of celestial charm they live in. Therefore he wished the children to be motivated to take interest in the literature and history of their own country and be taught the interesting and vitalising part of his own literature and the living and human parts of his nation's history.

Recognising that every person wishes to enquire, investigate, analyse and anatomise, Aurobindo included in his curricular programme the study of sciences which explain man's natural surroundings. He appreciated the austere discipline of science, of emotion-free intellect, which insists on putting everything to rigorous test and searches knowledge and truth. On account of his emphasis on man's mind and his psyche, he advocated the study of Psychology. To give an integral view of life, he stressed the inclusion of philosophy and logic. In view of the individual's natural power of imitation and imagination he wished the child's faculty of art to be developed appropriately.

Physico-vital Basis of Education

Analysing and elaborating his emphasis on the cultivation of right use of senses, Aurobindo concedes that some obstructions come in the way of the healthy functioning of the senses. According to him, these obstructions can be removed by the purification of the nervous system, which can be brought about by regulating breathing. It is a common experience that when we physically exert ourselves, our breathing becomes more rapid. This shows that the heart is more active and rushes blood through the arteries to make up the waste involved in the activity. But the regulation of breathing does not mean that we have to shun all work that entails physical exertion. Aurobindo wishes to emphasise that once the rhythm of inhaling and exhaling is established, all impediments to the free play of the life force would cease and there would be nothing to obstruct the report of the senses; the nerves would remain soothed and serene even under trying conditions. He, therefore, wishes the teachers to see that children remain alert to the importance of breathing which is the foundation of life in the living beings. This is of vital importance, especially in view of the fact that in our educational institutions every student has a sitting posture of his own and of a sort which invariably interferes with the free passage of air into his lungs from outside. The physico-vital basis of the students deserves immediate attention. He advises us to shake off sloth and inertia. He considers Brahmacharya (continence or conservation of energy) as the foundation of healthy life. Brahmacharya, in his words, "not only strengthens the 'medha' the grasping power, the 'dhi' or subtlety and swiftness of thought conception, the memory and the creative intellectual force, but enlarges, the range of mental activities."

Since Aurobindo considered "Yoga" as the main instrument of "self-perfection" of man, and wanted to create a community of perfected individuals for raising the standard of life of humanity, he advocated "Yoga" as a 'must' in education. Yoga to him, influences the mental, vital and physical being of man.

Moral and Religious Education

In the Education of the "whole-man" or "complete man", intellectual training is only one part. The other part and the major one is the development of man's moral and religious nature. Aurobindo says, "In the economy of man, the mental nature rests upon the moral." "Education of the intellect divorced from the perfection of moral and emotional nature is injurious to human progress." For him, the lack of moral and religious education tends to corrupt the human race. Both morality and religion relate to practical life. A mere study of moral consciousness, Aurobindo points out, is all theoretical and is not likely to have any influence on our way of life. Similarly a study of religion does not necessarily make a man religious. Morality consists in acting in accordance with the moral law. This requires the development of moral sense. More developed the moral sense is, the more inclined one would be to act according to the moral law. Moral life consists in controlling the impulses and instincts and forming wholesome habits, which bring well-being to one's self and order and security to society. According to Aurobindo 'moral nature has four components', emotions, formed habits, formed associations and innate nature. The child, therefore, be guided to cultivate right emotions, noble habits, right associations and his nature should follow right action. Moral education is education of the heart. As in the education of the mind so in the education of the heart, the, best way to help the child is to put him on the right road to his own perfection and to encourage him to follow it. He says, "The old Indian system of Guru who commanded, by his knowledge and sanctity the implicit obedience, perfect admiration, reverent emulation of the student was a far superior method of moral discipline. It is not possible to restore the ancient system but it is possible to have a wise friend, guide and helper teacher". For moral training, he prefers suggestions to impositions, example rather than precept. "The child should be given an opportunity to put into action his moral impulses that arise within him." For the purpose of moral training, children should be accustomed to that discipline by which they mould good habits and learn the notions of right and wrong. This would help them to keep to the right path in their later life.

He examines this question in two situations — English Boarding School and in the Indian context of ancient India. In the former the master appears at his best, leaving the boys largely to themselves to develop through mutual help and fellowship by following the path suggested to them. For the system Aurobindo remarks, "This method, though useful to a great extent, involves over much of outer discipline, which in the end becomes more or less mechanical. "Arid what is worse, fear becomes the basis of the pupil's respect for the law prescribed." As against this he considers the old Indian system of training under the guru superior. "The teacher in ancient India was a man of vast learning and sterling moral character. By his noble qualities he commanded respect and reverence from the pupil, who automatically emulated him." "But this" says Aurobindo, "is not possible because the teacher of that calibre is rare in India to guide the destiny of youngsters. The present-day teacher worn down by the earthly cares cannot take the place of the saintly teacher of the olden time." To make the best of modern conditions, Aurobindo emphasises the "method of suggestions" in imparting moral training. The teacher should suggest and inspire moral feelings and fervour in the pupils by personal example and by placing before them the lofty ideals of the past. Self-denial, thirst for knowledge, purity, chivalry, patriotism, large-heartedness and service can be stirred in the soul of the pupil more by personal character of the teacher than by anything else. The teacher must, therefore, be a man of integrity and noble ideas. "Moral training by the 'method of suggestion' can be supplemented by the application of an aspect of the kind of Yoga called 'Raja Yoga' which aims at the purification of the mind and the body. If any one has any bad qualities or propensities or bad habits both of mind and body, he will do well to adopt the method of "rejection and substitution". The children should be encouraged and directed to analyse their bad qualities and bad habits and cultivate good qualities and good habits.

Equally vehement is his emphasis on religious education. Religion liberates man from slavery to wrong ideals. It emancipates man from falsehood and gives us the divine health of courage and nobility. For him the essence of religion is to live for God, for humanity, for country, for others and for oneself. All this is practical. Theoretical knowledge of some religious commandments may prove futile. No religious teaching is of any value unless it is lived. In his words it is "absurd to think that children can be made pious by teaching them dogmas and doctrines of religion. The attempts to make boys moral and religious by the teaching of moral and religious text books is a vanity and a delusion, precisely because the heart is not the mind and to instruct the mind does not necessarily improve the heart". Such trends make religion either mechanical or lead to bigotry and fanaticism. He says, "Religion is to be lived, not learned as a creed." However, he does not rule out theoretical religious teaching, which is concerned with spiritual tests and emphasises the use of spiritual exercises, like meditation, rites, prayers and ceremony. In the current context the latter suggestion is open to criticism because every religion has its peculiar beliefs, rites and ceremonies. Votaries of every religion think that their's is the only true religion.

His Fundamentals of Instruction

In the matter of instructional technique, Aurobindo developed it into a "science". Instead of talking in platitudes, he goes to the grass-roots. To him learning becomes a burden on the learner if it fails to transform him. He starts with a radical statement that "the first principle of true teaching is that nothing can be taught". There is nothing contradictory about it. This is an echo of what Plato said about the 'doctrine of reminiscence', that is "learning is recollection and represents no new attainment". Aurobindo views that 'nothing can be taught' meaning thereby that nothing can be imposed upon the mind of the learner from outside. He does not agree with Plato that an individual is born to the world with the knowledge of all knowable things, although he credits every individual with infinite spiritual potentiality. Anyway, he believes that "teaching affords an occasion for the inner being of the pupils to be stirred to function in relation to facts. In the knowledge situation consciousness (with its extensive range and subtle faculties) matters; any physical interference from outside with the inner-folding is out of question. The only thing that can be done in teaching is to direct the activity of the pupil's mind. But this directing is not dictating. Mind has a spontaneity and an urge for self-determination, which the teacher should stimulate".

His second principle of teaching is that "the mind has to be consulted in its own growth. All minds are not alike. Each mind has its own peculiar features, capacities and aptitudes. The teacher, therefore, has to reckon with the inner disposition and tendencies of his pupil. A pupil can by no means be educated on a model alien to his inner being. Nor can he be trained for any preconceived career. The neglect of this principle proves disastrous". His plea was that education should be in accord with the aptitude and ability of the individual. Meaningfully he remarked, "The child cannot be moulded according to the desire of the parents and the teachers. He must be left free to expand in terms of his nature. To force the child to abandon his own 'Swadharma' is to do a permanent harm to him to militate his growth and deface his perfection."

Unfortunately these days our education being tailored to make students fit for earning a living by following the professions and careers, desired by the parents who, by and large, with their children to grow into money-making machines. The parents do not in the least take into account the innate tendencies and aptitudes of their wards. Quite often round pegs are put in square holes. It is ridiculous that a potential jurist is admitted into an engineering college or a born poet may be asked to study sciences. This disregard of the pupil's peculiar bent of mind has marred many a career. Aurobindo said, "Everyone has in him something divine, something his own, a chance of perfection and strength in however small a sphere which God offers him to take or refuse." He wants that the teacher should help every pupil to find this sphere, develop it and make the best of it.

Aurobindo's third principle is "Work from near to the far from that which is to that which shall be". For planning an educational programme we should start with what we are. For this we have to look back into the past, which gives clues to the methods of moulding the present. In the words of Aurobindo, "The past is our foundation, the present our material, the future our aim and summit. Past, present and future form a casual nexus. Each of these has to be given a proper place in a wholesome scheme of education." Here by "the past", he means heredity and cultural heritage and by "the present" he implies the nature of the individual and the needs of the modern society.

Although Aurobindo himself was not the creature of his childhood and boyhood environment and grew in accordance with his own divine spark, as an educator he was both a hereditarian and an environmentalist as he believed that "the nature of the individual is determined by heredity, environments, nationality, his native land, the air he breathes and the sights and sounds he sees and hears. The individual is shaped by the environments — first family, then physical, social and national traditions. Every human child responds to the environmental stimuli in his own way". Exactly the same belief is expressed by the American educationist, John Dewey, who considers man as the creation of biological and social situation. This, therefore, has to be admitted that in order to ensure the natural growth and development of children, our educational programme must rackon with the fact as to how the child's mind reacts to the environment.

Following the idealist school of philosophy, for the 'education of mind, body and spirit' his entire stress was on "knowledge", the sources of which are senses, mental faculties and reasoning or logical faculty. Since the materials for thought or knowledge (that is impressions, images and ideals) accrue through five senses and 'Manas' (Mind), Aurobindo placed the greatest premium on the training of the senses and the full evolution of the mind. He calls 'Manas' or mind as the sixth sense and deplores that the development of this sense has never been included in the process of man's education. The full development of the sensitiveness of the mind creates सूक्षम् दृष्टि or subtle reception of images. By this development mind gives correct report to the intellect in order to enable us to start our thinking correctly. Man often looks at things with a bias which has crept into him because of his environment. A more developed mind interprets impressions without any bias. In order to be free from bias one must purify his mental and moral habits, that is one must attain चित्त शुद्धि (Purification of mind) through Yoga.

He wishes that the sense organs should be preserved by protecting them from diseases. The pupils must be taught how to observe things minutely, so that the senses may report correctly to the Manas, which interprets them. The quality of knowledge depends upon the quality of materials manipulated in the *Manas*. The teacher should enable the pupil to cultivate the right use of senses, which supply him the ingredients wherewith to build the fabric of knowledge. He wants the hand and the speech to aid the senses. If the hand can reproduce what the eye sees, the object viewed becomes clear. Similarly children must be trained to speak out their ideas as the effort of express means much inner activity. Free expression of ideas shows that they have been perfectly formed and systematically arranged in mind. His emphasis on the use of hand and speech clearly indicates his inclination towards what Gandhi advocated as the education of the hand and the role of the mother tongue in facilitating the educative process.

In mental faculties Aurobindo includes attention, observation, memory, judgement and imagination. He enjoins upon the teacher to develop the power of attention, which according to him does not mean only centring the mind on one thing at a time. He insists that through steady natural practice attention may be given to a number of things in such a way as to learn everything perfectly. He advocated the development of the power of double concentration, triple concentration and multiple concentration. He wishes the teacher to see that the student concentrates his attention on things in a gradually increasing number.

To him observation is a source where from memory, imagination, judgement and other mental faculties draw their material. Careful observation is one of the conditions of good memory. It plays an active part both in scientific investigation and metaphysical speculation. He regrets that the faculty of observation is very imperfectly developed in men because of the want of due care in the use of senses. The faculty observation must be removed by training the senses. Its development in children should be the chief concern of the teacher.

He does not agree that children possess weak memories. If they have, he asks, who has made them so? The teachers! The student should not be required to repeat the same lesson for a number of times in order to commit it to memory. This is a mechanical and unintelligent way of training the memory. Instead, the pupil should be encouraged to observe different things and concentrate his attention thereon in order to reach a judgement about the same. Thus he will acquire the habit of observing the similarities of things and their differences. This is what he wants the teachers to encourage.

Aurobindo believes that with the help of the power of observation, attention, judgement and memory the pupils can learn botany through flowers and plants, astronomy through stars, geology through earth and stones, entomology and zoology through insects and animals. According to him every scientific subject can be taught by the training of the faculties to observe, compare, remember arid judge various classes of objects.

To him the faculty of imagination is the most important and indispensable instrument of education, as it helps man to have insight into such inner functions as "idea" and "judgement". Children should be stimulated to stretch their thought beyond the given. Their mental faculties should be fixed first upon the ordinary objects of sense and then gradually turned on words and directed towards thinking. Aurobindo ascribes three functions to imagination, the forming of mental images, the power of creating thoughts and the appreciation of the soul in things, beauty, charm, greatness, hidden suggestiveness, the emotional and spiritual life that pervades the world. The teacher has to help the children to exercise these three functions.

Although an ardent advocate of intuition, Aurobindo lauds the reasoning power or the logical faculty. "Reasoning power is calm, measured and comprehensive deliberation. Such a faculty creates an accurate and careful scholar, a pragmatic rationalist, a sober critic and cautious politician". According to him accurate reasoning depends upon correct observation, adequacy of data and legitimacy of the conclusions drawn. The child should be made interested in drawing inferences from the facts and tracing cause and effect. He says that "faculty can be best trained by talks of the teachers on everyday experiences and their objects". That is the best way to make the pupils conscious of the relationship between things and of their implications for farther experience. For him the teaching of "Logic" is a must at the adult stage, though the beginning can be made with the children, who should be trained in the art of making judgements and inferences by encouraging them to think about some facts in their own experience.

The Role of Teacher in His Scheme of Education

Man loses his sense of direction when the compass of his soul is not magnetised by some great human star. Out of this a sobering truth emerges that in the ultimate analysis, the teacher is the kingpin in the educational machinery. No system rises above the teacher. If the teacher fails to click and does not deliver the goods expected of him, even the best conceived system of education fails to produce efficacious results. According to Aurobindo, "The teacher is not an instructor or task master, he is a helper and a guide. His business is to suggest and not to impose. He does not actually train the pupil's mind, he only shows him how to perfect his instruments of knowledge and helps him and encourages him in the process. He does not only impart knowledge to him but also shows him how to acquire knowledge for himself. He does not call forth the knowledge that is written, he only shows him where it lies and how it can be habituated to rise to the surface". This is what pragmatists and naturalists say. Aurobindo wishes the element of genius in the pupils to be recognised. The teacher should not stifle it by the routine work. The child should not be regarded as an object to be handled and transformed by the teacher as he wants him to be. A teacher is not like a sculptor who can carve out a statue out of block of marble. The material of the teacher is different. While the material of the artist is inert, the teacher has to deal with a living organism. He cannot interfere with his material. He can only by suggestion help it develop and shape itself. The teacher is only a guide and not an imposer. The individual is a self-developing soul. The business of the parents and the teacher is to enable the child to educate his self, to develop his own practical, intellectual, moral and aesthetic capacities and to grow independently an organic being.

Since Aurobindo laid great stress on the "Intuitive power", he considered that teacher as ideal or liberal who encouraged the development of this power by "eliminating the admixture of error, caprice and biased fancifulness", and allows the child "to grow into the way of his own perfection". However, he says, that in this development the teacher cannot do much. He has to be a guide, helper and stimulator because the pupil has to develop according to his own nature.

Relevance Today

Philosophers 'live' and 'express' for all times. They are not the 'men of the hour' and speak things ephemeral. They are men for all times and their ideas, which have the universality become the legacy of the posterity. Critically Aurobindo answered the questions: What is man? What should he become? and through what means should he become that? He built up his general philosophy on the fundamental idea that 'Matter' as well as "Spirit" are to be looked upon as real. A spiritualistic philosophy that totally neglects Matter is one-sided, as a materialistic philosophy, which totally ignores the Spirit. As a true philosopher he realised that to fly from Matter would be really to fly from Spirit. He was not an escapist. He declared that it is possible for man in this terrestrial life to attain complete Divinity. Divinity is not something which man can only win by cutting off all ties with body, mind and life and become merged in the Absolute. Real salvation, according to Aurobindo, came by remaining in the physical universe, continuing to dwell in the body and having communication with his fellowmen. He wanted the transformation of 'mind' into 'super-mind', 'man' into 'superman' thus wanting the emergence of a race of Gnostic Beings, who have shed all ignorance and are illumined by the light of knowledge. Is all this not relevant in the Indian society today, when it is facing crisis of values? Is not this the panacea for our present ills? The great inspirer of *magnmn opus* — The Life Divine must be heard in this hour of trial and tribulation.

It was towards this end that Aurobindo conceived his philosophy of education and argued for close and necessary integration of the aims of life and the process of education. He told man that endowed by God, man had enough resources within him to grow to the plane of 'superman'. His perspective analysis of education during the British rule is more or less still true today. A rational appraisal of our education today still reveals that there is much to be desired. We will stand to profit from the reformulation of educational pattern by incorporating Aurobindo's educational ideas, which resulted from the broad onsurge of modern science. It was his conviction that 'India must come to terms with the modernisation-process', but without losing touch with the original Indian genius, the cause of which he has vigorously pleaded.

His details regarding the analysis of mind, his suggestion for the improvement of mind and his rationale to reckon with the instruments of knowledge should serve as eye-opener to many a teacher, who are hypnotised by their traditional outlook and questionable Herbartian steps of teaching. The education of the mind is most significant in solving our problem of national emotional integration, the pre-requisite basis of which should be individual's integration by educating his mind and creating in him the right type of emotions. It is then that unity and harmony of the nation will accrue. Supermind will help this integration.

"Intuitive power" has not yet been grappled by the educationists in India. This is manifested in the genius and the gifted. In our educational system, there is no provision for the identification of the gifted and educating him accordingly so as to prepare him for higher dispensations in life both in the interest of the individual and the society. Many a gifted die unhonoured, unsung, and unwept. This faculty of intuitive power is so important that it cannot be left out of the educational process. This must be encouraged. The teachers have to develop liberal outlook towards the genius so that they may flower and blossom to their full bloom.

Aurobindo's principle "that the mind of the student should be consulted in its growth", has been actually accepted as one of the main planks of modern education, which advocates education according to 3 A's (Age, Ability and Aptitude). In the present times we stuff the memory rather than train it. His emphasis on observation, attention, imagination, judgement and memory commends a great measure of attention of the educators.

The intellectual training about which the modern education is so emphatic is only a part of man's being. Aurobindo's education of the "whole man" includes man's moral and religious consciousness. Is not Aurobindo correct in highlighting that "the lack of moral and religious education tends to corrupt the human race". Aren't we ignoring the moral and religious nature of man at our peril? In view of the growing nihilism in the modem youth, it is high time for India, hitherto pre-occupied with political and economic issues, to search their mind for spiritual blisses. Religious and spiritual awakening is our immediate necessity. When the divine force flows in us, we have no fear and brute-force will be replaced by soul-force.

Much that Aurobindo says about education is universal and of enduring importance. It is of eternal verity. His was an eclectic philosophy, idealistic in aims, realistic in approach, pragmatic in action and humanistic in ambition. Let us have this approach to education.

Deeper we probe into Aurobindo's educational ideas, more realisation we have that his was an educational philosophy born out of the Indian genius and suited to the Indian genius. For the work of the future, it is imperatively necessary to create a centre of thought and knowledge which should revolutionise the brain of the nation. A new centre of thought implies a new focus on education.

He has bequeathed a will, full of sincerity and hope. He wanted Free India to take an effective place among the world's free nations, India to play a large part and take a leading position in the new age, assuring political, social, cultural and spiritual future of humanity; to bring about a revolutionary movement to create a united India; to have increasing resort not only to her teachings but also to her psychic and spiritual practice and to individual perfection and a perfect society. In the words of Aurobindo, "Whatever numerous and difficult problems we face, we must not disguise from ourselves that a great inner as well as outer liberation and change, a vast inner and outer progress is needed if we are to fulfil India's true destiny." When the energy of the West is balanced by the calmness of the East, a balanced humanity will arise.

Shall India listen to his clarion call?

REFERENCES

1. Sri Aurobindo: *The Renaissance in India*, 4th Edition, pp. 6-27.
2. *The Life Divine*, Vol. I, 2nd Ed.
3. *The Life Divine*, Vol. II, pp. 1035-36.
4. *The Synthesis of Yoga*, First University Edition, p. 4.
5. *A System of National Education*; Arya Publishing House, Calcutta; pp. 3-12.
6. *Integral Education*; Compiled by Dr. Indra Sen, pp. 1, 3,4, 5 and 13.
7. Aurobindo: *The Brain of India*, pp. 7-8, 13,49 and 51.
8. D.S. Sarma: *The Renaissance of Hinduism*, p. 317.
9. *Karamyogin* — a weekly published by Aurobindo from February 12 to April, 1910.
10. Sri Aurobindo: *Complete Works of India*, Vol. 17 (The Hour of God and other writings), pp. 191-226.
11. Das, A.C.: *Sri Aurobindo and some modern problems*; General Printers, Calcutta; 1958.
12. Mitra, S.K.: *An Introduction to the Philosophy of Sri Aurobindo*; Benaras Hindu University, 1945.
13. Sri Aurobindo: *Lights on Yoga*; Arya Publishing House, Calcutta, 1944.
14. Purani, A.B.: Evening Talks with Sri Aurobindo, Aurobindo Ashram, 1961.
15. Haridas Chaudhry: *Philosophy of Integralism*, Aurobindo Pathamandir, 1954.
16. Pandit, M.P.: *Sri Aurobindo : Studies in the Light of his Thought*, Aurobindo Ashram, 1961.
17. Uttarpara Speech: Sri Aurobindo ; Aurobindo Ashram, 1950.
18. Haridas Chaudhry: *Sri Aurobindo : The Prophet of Life Divine*; Aurobindo Ashram,Pondicherry; 1960.
19. Letters of Sri Aurobindo: Aurobindo Ashram, Pondicherry, 1954.
20. Pandit, M.P.: *The Teaching of Aurobindo Study Circle*, Madras, 1959.
21. *Ibid.: Light from Sri Aurobindo*; Dipti Publications, Aurobindo Ashram, 1970.

9

Dr. Mohammad Iqbal

(NOVEMBER 9, 1877 —APRIL 21,1938)

"My forefathers were Brahmins. They spent their lives in search of God. I am spending my life in search of Man."

—Muhammad Iqbal

Saare Jahan Se Achcha Hindustan Hamara, an inspiring and patriotic poem, sung as one of the national anthems, was the sublime and elevating composition of Dr. Muhammad Iqbal, a renowned poet, a profound philosopher and committed patriot, of renascent India. A Kashmiri Brahmin by ancestry, this VOICE of Tuhid, Muhammad Iqbal was born on November 9, 1877 to a highly religious Kashmiri tailor in Sialkot. The mystic temperament of his father, caressing sentiments of his mother and keen solicitude of his first teacher (Maulvi Mir Hassan) find an echo in his philosophy, poetry and career.

Iqbal completed his Matriculation in 1893 and Intermediate in 1895 from the Scottish Mission School and College of Sialkot, winning the gold medals. He did his B.A. in 1897 and M.A. (Philosophy) in 1899 from Government College Lahore and won the first position in the Panjab University, Lahore. In his student days he acquired reputation of being a good poet. His poetry depicted his patriotism and the natural scenes, sounds and colours of nature in India. He was the poet of Muslim awakening and Indian awakening.

After finishing his education he became a Reader in Oriental College, Lahore and then Assistant Professor in Government

College in Lahore. In 1904 he wrote his famous poem "Sarre Jahan Se Achcha Hindustan Hamara" and next year he went to England to study Philosophy at Trinity College, Cambridge. From Munich University in Germany, he did his Ph.D. in Philosophy and became a Bar-at-Law. For a few months he taught Arabic at London University. He returned to India on the 27th July, 1908, started practising law in the Lahore Chief Court as well as taught philosophy in Government College, Lahore as a part-time professor. He was member of the Legislative Council from 1926-1929 and was invited to Round Table Conference twice in 1930 and 1932 in England. He died on 21st April, 1938.

His Philosophy

Education is the dynamic side of philosophy. The theoretical postulates of philosophy find their actual realisation in education. In other words philosophy is 'theory' and education is practice. Philosophy tells us what is life? What are its aims? How can these aims be realised? Education becomes the means of realising those aims. It is, therefore, essential that before we examine the educational ideas of Dr. Iqbal, we have to understand his philosophy.

There are philosophers who are "idealists", calling the physical or material world as illusory, fleeting, transient. They consider the mental or spiritual world as the real world, permanent and eternal. Again, there are realists who do not wish to go beyond what they apprehend and call physical or material world as the real. For them that alone is real, which is seen, experienced and felt. They do not believe in anything 'metaphysical' 'transcendental', or spiritual. Fortunately Dr. Iqbal believes in the happy amalgam of the two — the REAL and the IDEAL. He does not consider the two as mutually exclusive and "takes the real to be the starting point to reach the ideal. As an Idealist he wishes the individual to attain the highest richness of mind, not in vacuum but in the social milieu, by acting, interacting and reacting in the realities of the environment. He does not wish man to withdraw from the material world but to face the facts and forces of this and to strive for the heights of mind. He wants man to play the human drama to its perfect expectation on the stage of social environment. His advice is "to use the great resources of the material world to attain the highest spiritual world". He wants man to "look for the secrets of life in the bud but keep the gaze towards the rays of the sun". He affirms, "The relation of man to Nature must be exploited in the interest, not of unrighteous desire for domination but in the nobler interest of a free upward movement of spiritual life".[1] Dr. Iqbal, therefore, wants the educator to take note (when formulating his policy and process of education) that "The ultimate REALITY is spiritual and its life consists in its temporal activity. The spirit finds its opportunity in the natural, in material and secular". He does not therefore wish to see "that the purpose of education should be to see that man does not subordinate the mental to the physical, concentrating only on the effort to gain the whole world even though he may lose his soul in the process". Philosophically Dr. Iqbal is concerned both with immutable and unchangeable world of 'spirit' as well as with the "world of changing phenomena" and wanted his "Developed Individual" to conquer the two worlds with his intellectual and creative activity. While he concedes that the Universe is real, serious and meaningful reality, he also adds that this universe is neither pre-determined, nor fixed or ready-made or immobile and incapable of change. He avers that it is a growing Universe, capable of infinite change and extension through the free and creative activity of man. He, therefore, wants the man to be up and doing.

Dr. Iqbal is Humanist to the core. His entire philosophy converges on the man, his nature and the development of his individuality in the social milieu. He was able to expand his concept of "momin" to make it co-equal with that of "man" itself.

His is a philosophy of action as is clear from

अमल से जिन्दगी बनती है, जनत भी जहनम् भी
न खाकी अपनी फितरत में नूरी है न नारी है।

In the words of late Dr. K. G. Saiyidan, "his entire philosophical thought is an eloquent plea for a life of strenuous activity and endeavour in which the self-interacts with its material and cultural environment. The Self-utilizes this process for creative self-expression in order to form greater purposes and to attain new reaches of power. He condemns life of withdrawal and passivity. Action is in his philosophy the pith of life. He was an experimentalist who did not wish the individual to be passive. He, therefore, wanted intense and manifold activity on the part of the child carried on in vital contact with group culture". For him, "the Intellect has been evolved in, and for the service of, Action. Intellect is a hand-maiden for the achievement of life's purposes:" Highlighting the primacy of life's purposes, he says, "we do not live to think, we think in order to live".

With this background of Iqbal's philosophy of eclecticism (culling wisdom and good points from idealism, realism, humanism and experimentalism) let us proceed to examine his concept of Man, Mind, Knowledge and Values, all the four being fundamental parameters of a philosophy.

Man

Analysis of the concept of man and his human nature receives the first attention of an educational philosopher. Perhaps no other philosopher has exalted 'man' as much as Dr. Iqbal. Being a deep rooted humanist, he stood "for the preservation of human personality", whose nature and function was elaborated by him in his Persian Masnavi, Asrar-i-khudi (The Secrets of the Self). Recognising Khudi (self-hood, individuality) as real and significant basis of life, he says that the negative of the Self, or its absorption into some Eternal self is not man's moral or religious ideal. Man should strive to retain his precious individuality and should strengthen it by developing greater originality and uniqueness in it." He wished ego-hood to reach its highest perfection. In man, he affirmed, there is creative impulse, which enables man to have unlimited growth and freedom. In his words, "Man has achieved the highest measure of individuality and is most conscious of his own reality. His ego (self) responds to other egos but his own ego still remains firm, positive and permanent and never immerses into any Absolute-self even when it wishes to have the highest ambition and bliss. He said, that "the self" is a reservoir of yet untapped powers and great possibilities. All these warrant that the individual should throw himself open to all kinds of formative and challenging experiences. "If he withdraws from the world of strife his individuality will shrink and wither and his powers will remain unrealised."

"Man", in his words, "can fully realise his personality if he throws himself whole-heartedly into the troubles and turmoils, the joys and sorrows of the world."

How does the individuality develop? Dr. Iqbal is emphatic in saying that the self or individuality or personality develops through "constant, strenuous effort and struggle against two things: (1) the forces of environment and (2) disruptive forces within man himself'. There is give-and-take relationship between the individual and the multi-dimensional environment. The individual, therefore, instead of remaining aloof from the environmental influences and thus becoming ego-centric, should have "intensive and fruitful contacts" with the environment and thus enrich his mind with the "energising currents of social life".

Dr. Iqbal considers the "formation of new purposes and desires" as an essential factor in the development of the individual. According to him, "Desire enriches life, gives meaning to life and disciplines the powers and actions of the individual. Desire is the sole capital with which the individual builds up the self, his culture and his institutions." In the words of Dr. Zakir Hussain, "Dr. Iqbal assured his generation that the true believer, the Man of God had the power to change the decrees of fate"[2] Dr. Iqbal exhorts man in the words, "Exalt thy ego so high that God himself will consult thee before determining the destiny".

खुदी को कर बुलन्द इतना, कि हर तकदीर से पहले
खुदा बंदे से खुद पूछे, बता तेरी रज़ा क्या है

"Dr. Iqbal's analysis of human nature and the individual's development has culminated in the portrayal of his GOOD MAN"[3] who

— leads a creative life of effort and struggle as a result of which he transforms the crude world into beautiful world

— applies his intelligence to the exploitation of the forces of nature

— lives his life in the name of the Lord, dedicating all his powers to the working out of His increasing purpose on earth. He subordinates everything to God.

— sets out on the arduous course of self-realisation and self-development.

— refuses to make compromises with evil or falsehood.

— develops all his powers and strengthens his individuality in active contact with his material and cultural environment.

— cultivates Courage, Tolerance and Faqr.

He firmly believed:

फरिश्ते से बेहतर है इन्सान बनना
मगर इसमें लगती है मेहनत ज्यादा

It is a better to be man than an angel, but it requires a lot of perseverance.

Mind

Like prophets and seers Dr. Iqbal extolled the wealth of the "world of mind" and rightly asserted that ''मन की दौलत हाथ आती है तो फिर जाती नहीं।'' (The wealth of mind once secured, is never lost). In Dr. Saiyidain's words, "Dr. Iqbal considered the goods of mind and the riches of the spirit, always aspiring upward in man, far too valuable". "Man's creativity should not only be confined to the reshaping of the material world alone, but should also build a much vaster world in the depth of his own inner being wherein he discovers sources of infinite joy and inspiration in art, poetry, literature, science, philosophy and religion." Enrichment of mind was his chief cult and creed. He wanted an open mind, taking, analysing and synthesising the impressions gathered through interaction with other minds as well as with the environment and the society. Dr. Iqbal pleaded "that the schools should attempt to elicit the intellectual, aesthetic and moral significance of the occupations and interests of life and to find the growing points of the mind in its effort to handle the every day concrete problems".

Knowledge

Highly concerned with the development of individuality through freedom and creativity, Dr. Iqbal has given a place of pre-eminence to Knowledge, which is experimentally acquired. In view of the present growing and fast changing environment, he thinks, awakening and cultivation of intelligence is essential and that can be done only through knowledge. He says, "The life of (finite) Ego or Self in an obstructing environment depends on the perpetual expansion of knowledge based on actual experience, which expands by the method of trial and error. It is through a spirit of intellectual adventure, through trial and error, through a fearless exploration into new realms of thought that we can make our original and valuable contribution to the enrichment of knowledge and consequently of life." He, therefore, "exhorts the learners not to be intellectually timid but to boldly conquer new domains of knowledge".

Values

While realisation of the values of "spiritual bliss" were considered by Dr. Iqbal as the acme of man, he wanted man to pursue cultural values and motifs of purely Indian origin. He was as much influenced by Indian Vedantism as by the teachings of Islam and the visions of Koran. These, he said, would "strengthen the upward movement of the human spirit. Like the idealists, he does not believe in any once-for-all fixed values. His values remain in progressive formation.

Since he is anxious to build a social order on the broadest humanistic lines he welcomes the social values which according to him provide a hope of society based on the principles of equality, social justice and human brotherhood.

In the light of the preceding discussions of Iqbal's philosophy of life, concept of man, mind, knowledge and values, we have now to examine the implications of education, as conceptualised by Dr. Iqbal.

Connotation and Aims of Education

The analysis of his eclectic philosophy (combining the good points of idealism, realism, humanism and experimentalism) gives a corollary, which considers education as the vital factor in moulding the "Man" of his imagination. He had an unflinching faith that man's individuality or personality' is something real, has creative impulse to grow, wishes to enjoy freedom and attain highest perfection. Evidently, helping the man to grow into his full stature was the most important task of education. Dr. Iqbal's ambition to covert 'Man into 'Mu'min" (true believer, the good man) led him to say: इलम का मकसद है पाकिये अकलों खिरद "The aim of education is purification of intellect and wisdom." He stressed that education should "strengthen the individuality of the educands so that they may realise their potentialities to the highest perfection. "The fullest development of 'Self or Individuality or Personality was considered by Dr. Iqbal as the greatest reward of man. He viewed "the cultivation of the individuality as the highest goal of all social and educational efforts."

That man should have "desires", "ceaseless quest for desires", more "desires" and visions of new horizons was the creed that Dr. Iqbal preached. He, therefore, wanted that education should aim at arousing, sustaining and perpetuating the quest of "desires" in the educands. New purposes and new desires could not be stimulated in a vacuum but through meaningful, positive and active interaction with the multidimensional environment — political, economic, social, cultural, moral and aesthetic.

Emphasising that "the perfect individuality results from the dynamic and stimulating environment "he wanted man to grow in the social milieu and enrich his mind by establishing a give-and-take relationship. The self-centredness of the individual will have adverse effect on the development of man's personality.

फर्द कायम रबत मिलत से है तनहा कुछ नहीं
मौज है दरया में और बेरून दरया कुछ नही

(Individual exists as long as he has social relations. Alone he is nothing, just the wave exists only along with the river).

Education should, therefore, aim not only at the individual development but also at the social development of the educands, which implies that they must have adjustment with the processes of the society. Dr. Iqbal averred,[4] "It is the lot of man to share in the deeper aspirations of the Universe around him and to shape his own destiny as well as that of the Universe by adjusting himself to its forces as well by putting the whole of his energy to mould the forces to his own end and purpose. "And, in this process of progressive change, God becomes a co-worker with Man, provided man takes the initiative. If he does not take the initiative, if he does not evolve the inner richness of his being, if he ceases to feel the inward-push of advancing life, then the spirit within him turns into stone and he is reduced to the level of dead matter." It is education, which ignites the *creative process* of man and constantly goads him to "play an active role by purposefully acting, interacting or reacting to his environment". This was the second aim of education, which Dr. Iqbal affirmed time and again.

His third aim, spelt out for education was that the educands must recognise the "value of community's culture", which implies that the educands should not only critically appreciate the cultural achievements of the community but must also "adhere to the highest of its cultural values and traditions. Any form of education which ignores this fundamental task is utterly superficial and futile". Dr. Iqbal resented 'the slavish imitation of the ideas and culture of other people which weaken the "Self". The individuals as well as the community should develop self reliance and inner richness of their own". This is where education should help. Iqbal said.

"Look into thy own clay for the fire that is lacking.
The light of another is not worth striving for."

He deplored the slavish imitation of the Western culture and practices by the Indians and advised his own son Javid, as the representative of the rising generation, that

"Do not take the obligation of the glass shop of Firangi
Create your own cups of wine from the earth of India."
उठा न शीशा गरान फरंग के ऐहसान
स्फाल हिंद से मीना औ जाम पैदा कर

Dr. Iqbal himself having patriotic impulses, was sad to see Indian youth having become denationalised through an education (given by the British to India), which ignored Indian past history and culture and did nothing to strengthen their individuality or stimulate their originality. He was, however, appreciative of some of the "valuable contributions of the West, particularly their spirit of research, their sciences, their strenuous efforts to gain control over their environment". Only he hated "the superficial and sensational side of the activities of the West which gave a false sense of being modern and progressive". He wanted the Indian youth to be "courageous and self-reliant".

In unequivocal terms he advocated the cause of Moral Education. This was his fourth aim. In the perfectly developed individuality or personality, Morality was a "must" for Dr. Iqbal, but not the morality, which is rigid and superimposed. "Education cannot produce genuine moral behaviour by teaching a set of ready-made moral maxims, which students may carry out mechanically." He wanted the moral code, which "arises out of a willing co-operation of free-egos". For him "goodness is not a matter of compulsion". Effective morality results from choice, freedom and experience gained through social intercourse. It implies that schools should provide opportunities for social experience.

Curriculum

Dr. Iqbal wanted a life-centred curriculum, realistic and related to the needs and demands of the developing individual and also reflecting the norms, nuances, values and aspirations of the society. He wanted subjects, which should help the educands to have all-round development — physical, social, economic, cultural, moral and spiritual. Recognising sciences as "instrument for the reservation of life", he wanted these to be taught but controlled by faith in ethical principles, because he saw that uncontrolled by ethical principles "sciences had given to Europe an inhuman economic system, an unjust social organisation a bitter conflict among groups and classes, a craze for armaments, a perpetual threat impending wars, a life of hurry, strain, frustration and distaste for quiet enjoyment of the fruits of culture. Tremendous powers which science has released and placed at the disposal of man should be used for human purposes. It will give to man not only sovereignty over Nature but the control over the scientific method through which he can explore and consciously reconstruct his world."

In view of the science not being capable of giving man a complete idea of Reality, Dr. Iqbal advocated the imparting of religious education, as he firmly believed that science and religion, instead of opposing each other, complemented each other. "Religion", according to him, "has always elevated the individuals and transformed whole societies." To him "religion in its higher manifestations is neither dogma nor priesthood nor ritual. It prepares man for the burden of the great responsibility." Education should, therefore, impart religious education, which helps man to "understand and appreciate modern, social, political, scientific or philosophical problems". "Living nobly arid adventurously in the name of the Lord" is the religion advocated by Iqbal.

Realising the power of the past in the true understanding of the present, Iqbal gave a place of honour to the teaching of History and historical evolution. Concept of history was, however, not "just an amusing story or a legend, recounting interesting happenings of bygone days. It should vividly recreate the past, mirror the sources and achievements of the peoples' culture and give them a true understanding of their place and function in the general march of mankind. The living assimilation of past history should give them a fresh sense of power and self-confidence and strengthen their individuality."

Simultaneously he prescribed the study of Cultural Heritage as "the people can gain new vitality and inspiration by turning to the healthy sources of their past culture." He wanted that we should be appreciative of the role of original, creative individuals in the development and progressive reconstruction of the life of a community. The social order always tends to be stable. The individuals with independence of thought and originality of vision give the society new values and dynamic urge."

Iqbal wanted education to cultivate Courage,. Tolerance and *Faqr or Istighna*; Courage to eradicate those influences which tend to produce an attitude of Fear; Tolerance for others, opinions and beliefs, their thought and behaviour; and Faqr to retain an inner attitude of detachment and superiority to material possessions, a kind of intellectual and emotional asceticism. In the words of Dr. Saiyidain "Dr. Iqbal exhorts the youth to build in themselves a fuller and worthier life of high idealism, undaunted courage, a sense of justice and an attitude of *Faq*[5]."

Instructional Technique

"Freedom" was Dr. Iqbal's watchword in the educative or learning process. He was of the firm view that "life cannot unfold all its possibilities, nor can the individual develop all his latent powers, except in an atmosphere of freedom, which (a) allows unchecked experimentation with environment; (b) encourages choice and discrimination in the use of methods and materials; and (c) motivates learning by direct personal first hand experience." In this way he wanted the schools "to bring up free, daring and creative individuals, not emaciated hot-house plants, not youths who have been kept in leading strings". He said:

> Imprisoned life is reduced to a small rivulet
>
> Free, it is like the boundless ocean![6]

"The freedom of choice" Iqbal said, "is the distinctive gift to man alone. This gift helps him to develop his personality and participate in the creative life of his Maker." He visualised the risk of freedom of choice, which man may use in choosing good or the opposite of good but Iqbal said, 'That God has taken this risk, shows His immense faith in man, who must justify this faith by a wise and constructive use of this gift".[7] He reiterated several times that, "unfolding of man's latent possibilities, his creativity and originality sprout in the atmosphere of freedom. Deprived of freedom man becomes a slave and as one incapable of original creative activity."

For teaching he approved of only those methods, which involved self-activity, learning by doing, problem solving, purposeful work experience where the students utilize the resources of their environment, adopt appropriate means to realise the goals and "rely on their own groping with intelligent efforts and overcome their difficulties". "Knowledge divorced from activity is apt to become dead and superficial" asserted Dr. Iqbal. Although he has not specifically mentioned the name of Project method, but when he advocates purposeful activity, he hints to project method, where purposeful activity is carried on in a social setting and where there is "the awakening of the questioning attitude".

Providing concrete experience to the learner was Dr. Iqbal's great maxim. In the words of late Dr. K.G. Saiyidain, "Iqbal ridiculed the school-master who wants to bring up children like hot-house plants, deprived of the educative and stimulating contact with Nature."

Dr. Iqbal, very specifically and pin-pointedly lays down as to how to educate children on sound principles of psychology. He averred,[8] "It is difficult to teach the innocent children and our teachers do not have the full cognizance of this problem. They do not adequately take into consideration the learnability and the intellectual capacity of the children. The children's faculties remain in disuse and their faces do not radiate that gaiety, which is the characteristic of this stage of life. As a result thereof, they in later life do not understand the problems of life and their solutions, which are essential for a practical man."

"In fact education of children is the indication of national progress. If their education is conducted on sound principles their life will be happier and effective. An appropriately educated child shows through his behaviour as to how he can lead an honest life. A child's intellectual horizon should be widened so as to cultivate his mind to its full richness. Bereft of any moral strings, they grow selfish. A man should be aware of his obligations and conscious of the fact that he is like a branch of a big tree, the roots of which are in the earth and its twigs touch the sky. To produce such a perfect man it is essential that children's character, education and training be well conceived. The society which ignores this, is unjust to the children. One should know the educational principles of educating the children and help them to discover their potentialities, thus formulating their education and training in conformity with their potentialities". He said, "If the mason lays his first brick wrongly the entire wall will remain infirm. Dr. Iqbal has spelt out eleven principles to be kept in view while educating the children:

1. A child is keen for activity. His surplus energy must get outlet. This must be utilised. A child is a dynamic entity. Every childish act of his can be exploited for educational purposes. All his activities of mirth and song be sublimated into constructive and creative acts.
2. Children cannot attend to a thing for long. He wants variety in activity. This trait of the children can be taken advantage of by the educator, who should divide his lesson into "units" in order to sustain the attention of the children.
3. Children take interest in observing and touching things. So much so that a small infant is curious to catch the flame. He wants to possess everything that he sees. The educator can develop his power of observation and train his senses by bringing him into contact with actual objects.
4. Children are attracted towards bright colours. The educator should, therefore, develop his colour sense.
5. Children imitate the elders and learn things from their parents. They are interested to do mono-acting and wish to play the role of a teacher or a shopkeeper or a hawker. Teacher should always present a good model so that they may imitate good things.
6. The power of imagination and thinking in the children is highly pronounced as is clear from the fact that they begin to pester their grannies to tell them tales and fables. The teacher should take full advantage of this trait of the children.
7. Children's natural habit of being sympathetic can be utilised by the teacher in inculcating moral education among the children.
8. Children have wonderful memory for vocabulary and remembering things. The teacher should always try to encourage them to remember verses and poems.
9. Since their power of judgement and discrimination is not highly developed at this stage the teacher should present different objects and sharpen their power of judgement by giving them comparative view of these objects.
10. Their power of logic is not very strong. They should be given exercises which create this characteristic in them. Give them

comparative situations and their power of discrimination would sharpen.

11. With a view to teach them morality the teachers should create situations of morality in the activities from the very beginning, They should be taught how to be sympathetic, how to be attentive to their lesson. The psychic development as well as the biological development should take place simultaneously.

If the future generation is to be made patriotic and hard working the teacher should inculcate in them the moral, cultural and religious virtues.

His Visions

Symbolising the best of the composite culture of India, Iqbal, a poet, philosopher, patriot and educationist — all in one — remained in perpetual quest for "Perfect Man". He said, "My forefathers were Brahmins. They spent their lives in search of God. I am spending my life in search of Man".

His writings abound in the pangs of troubled soul, seeking to understand BEING in relation to the society and the universe. To him "Life acquired the highest status when fired with promptings of self. Existence without the flame of (highly developed) self is mere breathing of a mound of clay". To him Man is the roof and crown of all creations of God. ACTION by man was given a prominently prime place. For this Man of Action, he wanted dynamic and creative education, which,

— directs the nurture and release of the creative spirit of in man
— equips him with the desire and capacity to conquer ever new realms of art and science, knowledge and power
— inspires an optimistic faith in the destiny of man

He dreamed of new world order for the whole humanity, where the strong are just and the weak secure, a world based on moral order and governed by moral values. Like Juvenal he felt pain for the afflictions of the contemporary society. Like Horace Mann, he gave it a new soul and moral purpose.

In the words of Pandit Jawahar Lal Nehru, "Sir Mohammed Iqbal's position as a poet and a philosopher is far greater than that of the passing politicians of the day. It is right that we should pay homage to his memory and seek inspiration from his writings."

REFERENCES

1. Lectures undertaken at the request of the Madras Muslim Association and delivered at Madras, Hyderabad and Aligarh.
2. Iqbal's Conception of Good Character as interpreted by late Dr. K.G. Saiyidain.
3. Dr. Zakir Hussain: Presidential address to the Seminar on Religion and Society at the Indian Institute of Advanced Study, Simla, Oct. 20,1975.
4. Lectures.

   Lecturer I. (Knowledge and Religious Experience), in the Reconstruction of Religious thought in Islam by Sir Mohammed Iqbal: Kitab Publishing House, Delhi, p. 12.
5. Dr. K.G. Saiyidain: The Conception of Good Character, 1938.
6. Translation by Dr. K.G. Saiyidain.
7. Seven "Lectures" by Dr. Mohammad Iqbal.
8. Free and flexible translation of Dr. Iqbal's Urdu article: "Bachhon Ki Talim" in MAKHZAN, Jan., 1902.

10

Dr. Zakir Hussain

(FEBRUARY 1897 — MAY 3,1969)

To the greatest fortune of the Indian Republic, the first three Presidents, Dr. Rajinder Prasad, Dr. Radha Krishnan and Dr. Zakir Hussain were distinguished educational philosophers rather than politicians. Dr. Zakir Hussain, born on 8th February, 1897, was hardly 9 years old, when his father died and he along with his three brothers returned to their ancestral home Etawah in Uttar Pradesh (U.P.). After finishing his schooling locally, he joined the M.A.O. College, Aligarh. While he was studying in M.A., he responded to the clarion call of Mahatma Gandhi for non-cooperation with the British, boycotted the college and founded an institution, known as Jamia Millia Islamia in Aligarh. But to satiate his thirst for higher education, he went to Berlin University, wherefrom he earned in 1922 his Ph.D. degree in Economics. On hearing the disquieting report about the contemplated closure of Jamia Miliia for lack of funds, he returned to India in 1926 and took over as Vice-Chancellor of the JAMIA (then shifted to Delhi), which institution he developed for 22 years. In 1948 he joined the Aligarh Muslim University, which he ably administered as Vice-Chancellor for 8 years. During this period he was nominated as a member of Rajya Sabha in which capacity he continued until he was appointed in 1957 the Governor of Bihar. Five years later in 1962 he was elected as Vice-President of India. The year 1967 saw him elevated to the Presidentship of India. With a sense of elation he said "My choice of this high office has mainly been made on account of my long association with the education of my people. It is a great honour indeed that the nation has bestowed on a mere teacher who some 47 years ago resolved to devote the best years of his life to national education. In this new opportunity of service, I shall do my utmost to take our people towards what Gandhiji strove restlessly to achieve; a pure life, individual and social, an insistence on the means of being as pure as the end, an active and sustained sympathy for the weak and down-trodden, and a fervent desire to forge unity among the diverse sections of the Indian people".

Undoubtedly Dr. Hussain was thorough-bred, most creative educationist, who enriched education's "purpose as well as contents, experimented in methods and techniques, elucidated its true relationship not only with the national past, present and future, but also with the precious legacy of men as a whole. He has, on the one hand, shown sensitiveness to its social and psychological foundations, and on the other, been deeply involved in its moral and spiritual implications".

His Philosophy

To start with Dr. Hussain was an Idealist. A clear evidence to this is his zeal to translate Plato's *Republic* in Urdu. This kept him aglow and he is considered Plato with difference. He transcended narrow theological distinctions.

"Belief" to him was essential prerequisite of character. He said, "Feeble beliefs must be replaced by' healthier habits and irrelevant institutions by progressive institutions. "Our 'will' should get guidance not from the twilight of the intellect but from the broad-day light of true belief."

Secularist to the core, he was a Humanist with a broad vision and never allowed his Islamic principles and his nationalism fall into narrow grooves but set them in the context where the East and the West, the ancient and the modern, the Muslim and the non-Muslim could find a happy meeting ground. In the words of Frank Moraes, "He loved India, he loved the world. He loved Germany, not the Germany of Hitler but Germany of Goethe and Max-Muller." He loved truth, justice and humanity. He advocated humanistic education, the foundations of which are best laid in the early years of life.

In the context of education, a philosopher's thinking can be examined in terms of five parameters, *viz.* his concept of Reality, Man, Mind, Values, and 'Knowledge.

Reality

Being an idealist, he believed in the Reality of two worlds, the material world and the spiritual world. That is this universe is like a living organism, having body and soul. The material world or world of senses is the body of the universe and the spiritual world is the soul of the universe. Primarily it is the soul, which moves the universe. The material world is apprehended through senses and through the study of sciences. The spiritual world is the real world of eternal nature and is apprehended by mind, which is a primary and final reality and central core of the personality. While the world of senses deals with 'substance', the world of soul, explains the 'essence'. Spiritualism is realised by ideas, which are born in the mind of man. He wanted the realisation of the spiritual world and not to have the craving for material things.

Man

Dr. Zakir glorifies the child and idolises the MAN in order to develop man into what Eduard Spranger called "Social Type of Man" — one whose dominating mental trend is the love and service of his fellow men. For him the love and service of Man was not a man's religious and moral duty, which requires a conscious will and effort but the very law of his being, which works independently of consciousness or will. He credited 'man' with decisive power, which helps man to make efforts and achieve success. Service of man, regardless of distinction of caste or creed was his first article of faith. He wanted an economic order in which barriers do not exist between the rich and the poor.

While existentialists want to produce an "authentic man", Dr. Zakir wanted a "cultured man". It pained him to see that man has become creature of the environment. In his words, "The average individual has no self, no inner identity, nothing in him that can be esteemed as unique." He wanted to resuscitate the pristine glory of man. Education, therefore, he said, "must give moral purpose to man's life, his institutions and to the State as a whole".[2]

Mind

Mind, he said, should be so developed that it "exercises itself to tap its resources and enlarge its powers so that it may utilize its capacities in every field of knowledge and at every stage of education and of life".[3] He strongly urged the cultivation of Mind through the "goods of culture". A highly cultivated mind, he believed, would bring about a balance between the material world and spiritual world. Looking at the amazing advance of science and technology, which could create a heaven on earth or pull out the last flicker of human existence, he wanted these powers to be placed under the moral social supervision and linked with human values so that man's mind should have peace.

Values

Himself being an epitome of higher principles and values, he wished every one to have pursuit of excellence in life. He stood for the best values and norms, of Indian culture and tradition and commended values like selfless service, secularism and democracy. In his words, "Education in the truest sense of the word should help the mind of the educand to experience absolute moral and intellectual values"[4], which may be realised in the best way "in his work and in his life". "The allegiance to higher values", he affirmed, "has to be given not only in individual life, society also should own allegiance to them. The values derived from potent 'goods of culture' bring about a good and just society, a clean political life and an honest leadership devoted to the general good."[5] His higher values included the True, the Beautiful, the Good and the Holy, quite distinguishable from the values attached to Physical Health, Material Gain, Pleasures of the Senses and Sensual love. The values of the higher order have a sense of permanence, absolute worth and validity. They are detemining forces in life. Man's animal nature drives him to material values. His moral and spiritual being propels him to absolute values, which lend meaning and content to life. To develop these is the main task of education. Mind experiences these values through goods of culture, *viz.* science, technology, art and architecture language and literature, moral codes, great philosophers and personalities etc. etc.

Knowledge

Knowledge is great power for the cultivation of the mind and for insight into goods of culture. It is, therefore, essential that we must keep abreast with knowledge. Dr. Zakir Hussain wants two types of knowledge: (1) knowledge of substance, which science gives, and (2) knowledge of essence, which "involves knowledge of the qualities, of the purpose, the origin and the end of the object".[6] Such a knowledge is given by social sciences.

In the above perspective of Dr. Zakir Hussain's philosophical fundamentals, we have now to examine his concept and connotation of education, aims of education, curriculum, instructional technique and discipline. Dr. Zakir Hussain's concepts of an 'educated man', 'an ideal teacher', 'an ideal school'; his love for children, his contribution to Basic education, 'his philosophy of work', and his 'Jamia Millia Islamia' are also being discussed.

His Concept and Connotation of Education

That "education is the basic instrument of national purpose" sums up his total view of education. In the words of Saiyidain, "Dr. Zakir Hussain was of the view that a general and broad-based national renaissascence cannot be ushered in through the narrow gate of politics. It must have its moorings and draw its inspiration from education and culture". His concept of education was not putting information into an otherwise empty head. No, education is not dressing up, it is not writing on a *tabula rasa*. It is not the imposition of just this system or that system decided arbitrarily or in obedience to certain political ideology".[7] To him education is not mere learning of 3 R's, but is gradual initiation to the production of an ideal man through ideal system of education, which exudes democratic form of living and offers equal opportunities to all. He advocated universal education and no deprivation for the less privileged.

His devotion and exponential role in the cause of Basic Education propounded by Mahatma Gandhi arose from the deep-seated conviction that "education in a poor country must be related to the needs of the poverty stricken millions in the villages.

Dr. Zakir did not subscribe to "education", which has single-point entry and single-point exit. He pleaded for education for life or continuing education. He averted that "those who think that after coming out of colleges and schools their education concludes and they do not need any further education are thoroughly mistaken. The objective of education is not merely that children be taught reading and writing in the schools or be taught some selected books in the colleges and universities. There are not only two or three frontiers of education but providing many opportunities for keeping fresh their knowledge and great objectives."

His concept and connotation of education has been crystalised in his identification of Educated Man, who he says:

— has breadth of intellectual horizon concerning values attached to things and persons. He has no blinkers.

— possesses a certain degree of open-mindedness and accessibility to new values and ideas. He is no philistine.

— has an inner urge towards moral growth and constantly presses towards perfection in his own person or in the world around him.

— is not conceited and never imagines he has reached the destination.

— has a flexible and versatile relation to value-relationships among things as against the rigorous stiffness of the zealot or the bureaucrat.

— has his value-estimations organised round an absolute objective value and gives clear evidence of a central psychic focus which irradiates all his action, thought and feeling. He is no internally dissipated busy-body.

— maintains positive attitude towards the "goods of culture" that is, towards the ultimate objective values.[8]

He affirmed that such attitudes are the cherished product of educational and instructional activity.

Aims of Education

With a view to produce a harmonious and integrated personality, he wanted education to aim at all-round development — physical, intellectual, social, moral, spiritual and aesthetic — of the educand. He wanted education to raise the level of culture of the learners, through the "goods of culture" which he said, "give real nutrition to the mind through educationally productive work". He wanted the educand to be socially adjusted and conscious of the responsibilities of real Indian citizenship. He kept in view the totality of educand's being, whom education must help to realise his values, ends and interests. True education should foster in children the moral and intellectual values, goods of culture as well as aesthetic and religious interests.

He emphasised the Social Aim of education. 'Individual development' was his cardinal aim of education but he did not want individual development in isolation from the social milieu. He thought "poorly of a scholar who was morally indifferent person living by himself in a world of his own or of a person who was aesthetically unschooled and morally infantile. There are partial and socially ineffective or useless men. Community is the real elementary thing, while the individual exists through it and for it". He advocated socially-oriented education. His own institution the Jamia was "one of the first institutions to try the project method, to develop a community approach in living and learning, to encourage self-government amongst students and train them for responsible citizenship, to arouse interest in art, and above all inculcate in the students and the teachers a spirit of idealism and social and national service".

Himself symbolising integrity and secularly Dr. Zakir Hussain stood for education for National Integration and national synthesis through the development of social values and national conscience. Education, therefore, he averred, should aim at creating sensitivity to national integration. It should be converted into an effective social force. He said, "Persons who were engaged in productive, mental or intellectual work devoid of social content will grow into partial and socially ineffective and useless men."

In view of the India building a structure of democratic living in a secular welfare State, Dr. Hussain wanted education to aim at fostering national ethos in the individual, so as to enable him to contribute to the design of national life with his initiative, self-discipline, co-operation and tolerance,[9] He wanted every Indian to be patriotic without being a chauvinist.

Feeling sore at the "increasing disregard for human and moral values in the youth due to a growing estrangement with religious traditions", he strongly urged for Religious Education which was being excluded from schools and colleges. He said, "Education does precious little to correct this situation. No effort is being made to distinguish between the religion that seeks to divide humanity and the religion that gives meaning to life. The religious spirit is the fountain-head of the aspiration of Man to serve his fellowmen, to establish equality and justice; and to abolish ignorance, pain and sorrow. Man requires peace without and peace within. Even in a secular society, tolerance in matters of religion is a necessary civic virtue. Intolerance is unsocial."

Curriculum

Dr. Zakir Hussain did not wish that every one should study the same thing uniformly. He said, "To hammer into shape an educational ideal, considering it valid for all, is absolutely hopeless enterprise. In a democratic society the individual aptitudes should be developed and helped to grow so that the individual may evolve into a morally free and autonomous personality.[10] He, however, wanted that every one must know his own language besides one or two other Indian or foreign languages. Taking cognizance of the achievements of science and technology, he advocated their learning if handled properly. Along with natural sciences, he wanted the students to learn something of social sciences and vice-versa, because while natural sciences explain the 'substance' of the phenomena, social sciences give "essence" of the totality of the phenomena, that is what, how, whence, whither and why of everything in this world. He, therefore advises "science with ethics" and says "the concern of the science colleges is not only to send out successful engineers and technologists but also truly educated men. If an engineer can make machines, he should also be capable of enjoying good poetry, good book and good human relationship".[11]

Instructional Techniques

His cardinal principle was "learning by doing". His concept of doing was not merely intellectual but to a large extent spiritual. The intellectual element of this concept he had taken from German educator, George Kerchesteiner and spiritual element partly from Muslim mystics and partly from Mahatma Gandhi, blending the two with his own concept of "active education". He believed that education is the transmission of spiritual and cultural values of a nation to its younger generation in such a way as to make it an integral part of their life. These values are incorporated in the various organs of the cultural corpus of a nation, like religion, morality, science, art, etc. The educator has first to realise these values in himself and then to help his pupils in realising them. The sole effective medium of the realisation of these values is work. Thus religion can only be realised through religious practice, morality through moral action, science through scientific experiments and art through artistic activity". This principle was followed in Jamia — "a school of work" — where book-teaching was minimum and practical activity with an educational value was maximum.

Discipline

Dr. Zakir Hussain advocated self-discipline and not an imposed discipline and wanted "freedom" and "authority" both combined in a compromising manner. He affirmed, "The way to real freedom requires a good deal of directed effort. A school totally without direction and authority may prove to be a fruitless venture". He did not wish absolute authority, "uncritical acceptance, unquestioning conformity and training in mechanical fear".[12] Painfully was viewed by him the existing situation in India where "the students wish licence in what they do, giving evidence of their obsessions, dissipations and distractions. Along with this he saw the apathy and indifference of teachers which indicates that in this free land of ours the principle of wachsonlasson or 'Letting Grow' in any way is being conceded — if we cannot let them grow to bring forth flower and fruit, just let them grow into weeds."[13] Dr. Zakir never considered "freedom" and "authority" as opposite to each other. They are not contradictory but complementary to each other. The two have to go together because "there is no authority in education, which does not recognise inner freedom. Similarly there is no freedom without regulation and orderliness. Authority does not signify compulsion and freedom does not stand for licence and arbitrariness. There is no community, family, school, state — which prizes freedom and has no rules and regulations recognised as binding. There is no autonomous personality having no principles. Without regulative principles society would be a chaotic jumble".[14] Very aptly he said, "The road to freedom is made by authority. To cut out authority altogether would be to cut out that road." Authority, he affirmed, is essential both at the beginning and at the end of education. At the beginning it is required for correct guidance and helpful direction. At the end it is required because of the emergence of value, accepted for self-direction. There couldn't be more well-reasoned concept of 'discipline' than the one Dr. Zakir has left for the posterity.

An Ideal Teacher

Natured and nurtured in Idealism, Dr. Zakir Hussain's image of an ideal teacher was very high. Such a teacher is one who:[15]

- guides, helps and directs the young so as to develop in them a sense of responsibility for their actions;
- awakens in them an urge towards self-education;
- gives them the fullest measures of freedom and self-determination;

— transmits to them higher values through his personality and through the goods of culture and gets the values realized by them;

— does not dictate or dominate but helps and serves, understands and shapes in Faith and Love and Reverence; and

— recognises that the individual is not just a unit of calculation, an identity card or member but is to be helped to grow through work, knowledge and experience.

He made an impassioned appeal to the teacher, "not to always wait till others think out things and he sets out mechanically and soullessly to execute them. Let us evolve a healthy professional opinion, a high professional sense of national duty. We are just not wage-earners. We have to breathe the spirit of the intellect, of morality and social responsibility into the work of the hand and to give to intellectual work a firm foundation of concrete, purposeful activity".[16]

Dr. Zakir was of the opinion that, "a cynic will not make a good teacher but one who loves the children and hopes that they will become the vehicles of good life. He helps them to assimilate their cultural heritage and to enrich it further. He gives every individual an opportunity to proceed at his own pace". He wants the teacher to be a Social Type, concerned about the moral improvement of the society. He is the custodian of the highest values created and cherished by his people. He has to help the bud into full bloom and not to make paper flowers to satisfy his whim and fancy. The growth of moral independent personality is the aim and the end of his endeavour. By his love and patience he can produce the proper adjustment between the group and the individual. He can help men to grow to walk together with joy and work together with zeal."[17] Dr. Zakir Hussain pleaded that "the entire teaching community in the country from the lowest to the highest should be homogenous whole, in terms of prestige as well as material conditions of work and life. Improvement of teacher's living condition is the first prerequisite for improvement of the quality of education".

His Ideal School

Like his image of an ideal teacher, Dr. Zakir Hussain has portrayed the picture of an ideal school, which truly understands the individuality of the pupil, having values, ends and interests and where pupil's stage of development is always kept in view. Such a school, he says, is concerned with the growth and development of the intellectual, the moral and physical side of the pupil and not only to some one aspect. It is a place of purposeful activity of educationally productive work, which involves consciousness of the problem, means of solving it and the plan and steps of accomplishing it satisfactorily. Such a school is a community in which individual accomplishment is related to social achievement. "Such schools" he says, "stands out as the embodiments of moral objectives and noble-minded comradeship to find out the worlds of nature and man, appreciate and create beauty, uphold the standards of clean life, work for the good of the school community, play for the team and play fair. Life in such a school becomes service and builds up character, generates social sensibility, delicacy of feeling and a sense of social responsibility. Such a school initiates in its pupils the process of self-education, of awakening in them the desire to grow into fine moral persons with a view to help the society to become morally better."[18]

His Love for Children

Wordsworth, the famous English poet said, "Children come with trailing clouds of glory from God's heaven, which is their home."[19] Dr. Zakir said, "Every child who came to this world brings along the message that God has not yet lost faith in Man."[20] To him child "is the most interesting thing in this colourful world of ours". Three agencies — the nature, family and school — help sound and healthy growth of the child. Nature does it in its own way — sometimes slowly and at another time rapidly. The family does help but does not have that sense of proportion in its methods of socialisation which it should have. Therefore, he wanted the schools to assume serious responsibility in training them. He deplored the indifference of the schools, which kill the vigour, enthusiasm and creativity of children and transform them into listless, passive and non-reacting conformists, subjected to heavy curriculum, dull routine and monotonous methods. Recognising the vital role of the schools, he wanted them to know the expectations of the family, the society and the individual and cater for them. The school must provide education suiting the different aptitudes and abilities of different children, each one of whom is an entity by himself. He wishes children to be treated like children and given education on sound lines, preferably through individualised instruction and not class teaching. "Teachers", he said "should be provided with the technique of such competent observation as will enable them to understand their pupils and direct their educational work in the light of this understanding. This is possible if "normally intelligent, understanding and loving intercourse between teachers and their pupils on the playing field, in excursions and mutually helpful productive work is consciously organised".

Ample testimony of his love for children is borne by his writing stories for children under the pen-name — Ruqayya Rehana (Rehana was his daughter who died at the age of 5 years). His children's story book Abu Khan ki Bakri aur Chaudah aur Kahanian (Abu Khan's goat and fourteen other stories) is well-known book. He believed in the "provision of a rich and stimulating environment for the children's personality to flower".

High Priest of Basic Education

Dr. Hussain acknowledged that "the entire framework of his educational thinking "was influenced by two persons — Gandhiji and the eminent German educator, George Kerschensteiner. Gandhiji expounded Basic education. Dr. Zakir Hussain gave content, meaning and practicability to the rough ideas of Gandhiji. His perceptive and profound mind could foresee the merits of Basic Education, which had the promise of integrated type of education through which the physical, mental, emotional and spiritual faculties of children could be drawn out and developed in a balanced way through craft- centred and creative education. While advocating the linkage of productive craft with intellectual work, he strongly emphasised "quality" both in intellectual and craft-work, cautioning against turning the schools into small factories of spinning and weaving.

Convinced of the inherent soundness of Basic education, his only regret was that "it has not been given a fair trial. The new ideas and methods of Basic system were packed and crammed into the steel frame of conventional mechanism and they met their death by suffocation". Asked if Basic education has failed, he replied, "No, Basic education cannot be said to have failed. I have personally experienced its principles worked out successfully. How could a scheme of education of far-reaching significance and based on such manifestly sound educational, psychological and sociological foundations be declared to have failed before it has really been honestly tried. It awaits being honestly tried."[21] Enumerating the causes of its tentative failure he said, "Its basic ideas have not been adequately elaborated. A requisite preparation to put them into practice has not been made. Those responsible for the implementation of the scheme have not applied themselves to the task with the required energy. The teachers and administrators have not received the requisite training. There is a dichotomy between Basic and non-Basic schools working at the same level, thus giving the evidence of a divided mind. There is absence of the proper and mutually understood relationship of Basic school with high schools and universities. In Basic schools we have not kept in view the essential educative conditions of work. There is no semblance of a spontaneous motivation in the child, who is ignorant of any personal or social purpose behind his work. He is told to do in a certain prescribed way and is denied the stimulated joy of a joint discovery with the teacher."[22]

In his view, if Basic education misfired, it was because, "a greater emphasis was placed on the forms and techniques, rather than the essential spirit of Basic education."

His Philosophy of Work

Work — useful, systematic, skilful work — was a passion for Zakir Hussain. He did not consider work as a mere instrument of teaching and learning, it was something far greater. Besides giving joy in life, "work" helped the individual find his fulfilment as a member of the society. It was by work that one could realise Truth and attain salvation. He averred, "All work is not educative. It is educative only when it is preceded by mental effort. You have first to plan the work in your mind, then to think out the ways and means of doing it, then to perform it actually, and finally to assess the results and compare them with the guiding plan. But even when all those four steps have been gone through, it does not follow that work would prove educative. It would certainly give some skill mental or manual, but skill by itself is not education. Only that work is genuinely educative which serves some values higher than our selfish ends and to which we are devoted. He who works for his own ends may become skilled; he does not become educated. In the service of values Man does not seek his own enjoyment but strives to achieve perfection in his work to improve his character and become a real human being. The educative quality can be found in handiwork as well as in mental work and both can be devoid of it as well". He emphatically repeated, "work does not mean the passing of time by doing any haphazard thing; it is not amusement; it is not play; it is work; it is purposeful striving. It yields joy, unparalleled and unsurpassed. Work is workship".

The Promising Laboratory: Jamia Millia Islamia

Any person with superior qualities of head and heart as Dr. Zakir Hussain could easily get an eminent position under the British Government, but he was so much disgusted with the soulless pattern of English education, that he dedicated his life to build an institution called Jamia Millia Islamia, which symbolises a new ideology and represents new and promising adventure in education. For more than two decades he and his colleagues worked on a shoe-string budget and on less than a pittance for themselves. He selected his staff and students for Jamia less on the basis of intelligence and ability (although actually they were no less of high calibre) and more on the basis of humanity and nationality.

Jamia was his laboratory to test, verify and validate his educational thinking. Here the wisdom from East and West was pooled. People of all castes and creeds were welcome. All the educational innovations like project method, community living, citizenship training, integrated curriculum etc. were effectively and successfully tried. The institution imparted education, which suited the genius of Indian people. All the educational thoughts of Dr. Zakir Hussain were enshrined in the concrete form of Jamia Millia Islamia, now enjoying the degree granting status of a university.

His Future Vision of India

Living in resurgent and fast changing India, Dr. Zakir Hussain, the illustrious son of Bharatmata envisaged a sublime vision of India, characterised by democratic trends and processes, freedom and justice — social, economic and political, provided the nation followed the Gandhian path morally and spiritually and Nehru's path of material and social advancement. Everyone then would live a life of dignity, self-respect and non-exploitation.

He visualised future India to be a magnificent country with values and norms worthy of emulation by other countries, rather than imitating the so-called educationally progressive countries, which themselves are having a second thought over their system of education. Dr. Hussain wanted an education which suited the genius of our country and not the one imported from another country and transplanted here. He said, "of our innumerable ills and troubles, there are very few which we can remove in a short span of time. "The country needs not the spurt of your blood, but the steady flow of your perspiration at all times. It needs work, silent and real work. Our future will be decided in the broken hut of the farmer, in the smoked roof of the worker's home, and in the village school. Political quarrels, conferences and congresses will decide only the matters of tomorrow and the day after, but the places I have mentioned will decide our fate for centuries."

His constant advice for our country was "work, work and more work, silent and sincere work, solid and steady reconstruction of the whole material and cultural life of our people. This work has two aspects; work on one's self and work for the society. They are mutually fruitful aspects of work. The work on one's self is to follow the urge towards moral development under self-imposed discipline. Its end-product is a free moral personality. This end-product cannot sustain itself without the society being as such. The individual cannot grow to its full perfection without a corresponding advance of the collective social existence. The dual (individual and social) effort of work will give our state a specific flavour. It shall work for providing to each citizen the essential minima of decent human existence. It shall fight against intellectual laziness and indifference to the demands of social justice. It shall eradicate all narrow corporate selfishness. It shall do all this as the willing acceptance of a moral duty, as joyfully undertaken ethical task. Let us combine our national life power with morality, technique with ethos, action with meditation, the East with the West. Let us keep in view the eternal and the temporal, an awakened conscience and skilled efficiency, conviction and achievement."[23]

In his personality and thinking Dr. Zakir Hussain represented the image of Dr. Iqbal's 'man of faith' and Gandhi's 'man of truth'. He proved that a good teacher with intellectual brilliance, warmth of heart and depth of feeling can as well be a teacher of humanity, can grace a *gadi* as well as win a place in the hearts of men. Out of the crucible of suffering and hardwork, out of the sustained effort to qualify himself as a good and inspiring teacher, by his devotion to the basic principles of Nai Talim of Gandhiji, and above all by the patriotic spirit with which he served, Dr. Zakir Hussain rose to the highest honour India can bestow on his children. In the words of Dr. Saiyidain, "He was an educational thinker with vital and original mind, who gave a new orientation to Indian education and contributed to the re-patterning of educational methods at primary, secondary and university levels."

"Dr. Zakir Hussain will be remembered not merely because he rose to the highest seat (President) this nation could offer to her best son, nor because he so ably interpreted the theoretical basis of India's educational objectives but because he showed courage to tell his countrymen that the peculiarity and greatness of a nation does not lie in becoming a carbon copy of another country, however alluring and magnificent that may be but in her striking a new path which may lead her straight to her cherished goals."[24]

REFERENCES

1. Saiyidain, K.G. *The Humanist Tradition in Indian Educational Thought*, p. 128.
2. Convocation Address at the All India Institute of Medical Sciences on 27-3-1965.
3. Speech at the Rajasthan University, Jaipur on 30-11 -1963.
4. Educational Reconstruction, p. 113.
5. *Ibid.*, p. 58.
6. Dr. Zakir Hussain's Convocation Address at the Indian Institute of Technology, Kharagpur on 10-3-1962.
7. *Educational Reconstruction*, y. 11.
8. Quoted from A.G. Noorani's book *President Zakir Hussain*: A Quest for Excellence.
9. *Educational Reconstruction*, p. 681.
10. *Educational Reconstruction in India.* Vallabhbhai Patel Lectures, Dec. 1958.
11. Convocation Address at the Tata institute of Social Sciences, Bombay on 9-3-1963.
12. *Educational Reconstruction*, pp. 60-61.
13. *Ibid.*, p.82.
14. *Ibid.*, pp. 61-62.
15. *Ibid.*, pp. 63, 93, 94.
16. *Ibid.*, pp. 95-96.
17. Speech at the University of Cairo in April, 1968.

18. Speech on Founder's Day of the Modern School, Delhi on 25 11-1962.
19. Educational Reconstruction, p. 52.
20. Dr. Zakir Hussain's speech in Jamia on 27-11-1946.
21. *Educational Reconstruction*, pp. 108-109.
22. *Ibid.*, pp. 58, 83, 84.
23. Speech on the assumption of office of President on 13-5-67.
24. R.P. Singh, *Dynamics of Indian Education*, p. 92.